# Understanding China

Learning from China's Past, Present, and Future

**Stefan Piech**

First published in 2020

Book design by Stefan Piech

This book is dedicated to my mother who always supported me,
unconditionally

# ACKNOWLEDGEMENTS

This book would have not been possible without the help of many. A special thank you belongs to Ilmira Murni, Stefan Kessler, and Yiyi Yao.

# CONTENT

# FOREWORD

## By Leon Witt

When I started working in the headquarters of a global car manufacturer in Stuttgart, I was amongst colleagues who had worked for the company their whole lives, some of them doing the same type of job for almost 40 years. Unbeknownst to them, their lives were the epitome of privilege. Making six figures a year on a 35-hour workweek with benefits the rest of the world could only dream of is a lifestyle which represents the comfortable and complacent bubble of Western societies ignoring the geopolitical change taking place right now. Despite China being the most important business partner for every German automobile manufacturer, applications for expat positions in the U.S. exceed those for China by a lot. When I started my Ph.D. in Artificial Intelligence at Tsinghua University, China's single most prestigious technical university based in Beijing, I was the only German student in my class. Pupils who are sent abroad for a cultural exchange favour the U.S. over China by 150:1.

Whether this lack of education about China is intentional or not, we can no longer afford to ignore the reality. In those 40 years that my colleagues spent doing the same job, China transformed fishing villages into megacities with skylines that would make Frankfurt blush. GDP per capita grew fiftyfold over that period. Yet the longer I spend in Beijing, the more cognisant I become of the gap between the West's perception of Chinese society and its truth. I never heard about China once in any of my history classes. We weren't taught that China had invented gun powder and the printing press long before the Europeans ever conceived of them. For the longest period in the history of human civilisation, China was the most developed country, both economically and technologically. With this self-realisation in mind, China is working towards escaping the shackles of its last centuries of misery in the hopes of becoming the strongest international player. Whilst the democratic system of the West is being tested under the Trump administration and by the lack of consensus of European Union members, China is looking to the future. By implementing its Belt and Road Initiative, China is spreading its influence across Southeast Asia and Africa without a proper counter strategy from the West.

It is therefore more important than ever to understand what drives this striving nation, its cultural and socio-ecological history as well as its strategy to become a superpower by 2049. The deep insights given into China's past, present and future throughout this book are a wakeup call to its creeping influence in our contemporary life.

# INTRODUCTION

C hina is a country that up until today is full of culture, history, and tradition. Emerging in the east under the rule of many dynasties and growing to a worldwide superpower, many of the cultural aspects of the past still affect the behaviour of people today, the way business is done, and the way problems are solved in day to day life.

The big question is how one can make sense of the numerous changes that are taking place in China and that influence many parts of the world. What makes China Chinese? Are white-collar workers in cities like Shenzhen and Shanghai a good representation of Chinese people or are the many remaining peasants in the rural areas the authentic Chinese? How can a communist country have no safety net for the rural poor and yet lift more than 800 million people out of poverty? Why is it that China, which many argue is capitalist instead of communist, has a single-party government?

These are just some of many questions that come up in conversations about China. China is as black and white as Gerhard Richter's 4096 colours. China has many facets and is full of diversity. This in fact makes China such a fascinating country.

The goal of this book is to introduce different aspects of the daily life in China and to help the reader understand Chinese culture and pragmatism through different, everyday examples. Throughout this book we will talk about many aspects that characterize China for what it is. We will look into many different aspects of daily life in China, spanning from areas like family all the way to transportation and the usage of technology and its impact on the life of billions of people.

Additionally, in order to better understand the present, we will begin with a deep dive into the cultural and historical backgrounds of China, see how these aspects came to be and their development over time. Over the years, China underwent many transformations which shaped the country in their own way. While some were temporary and left little to no marks, others still impact Chinese behaviours and culture today. We will further see how some aspects differ between China and other countries in the world. With all that knowledge about the past and the present we will risk to take a look into the future and try to develop an understanding of how these aspects might shape a future China. Consequently, the third part of this book is forecasting a possible future, based on the knowledge we have gathered in the first two parts of this book.

I had the great privilege to live in the north and south of China myself, and experience its culture first-hand. Nevertheless, be aware that this book is written through the lens of a foreigner and that aspects of my interpretation might be biased.

I encourage you to travel to China yourself to obtain a first-hand account of this fascinating country. Be it for travel or for business. It is my hope that this book can shed some light on the intricacies of Chinese culture.

When you travel to China for the first time, it is hard to miss the different aspects that we will talk about in this book. Stepping out of your airplane and making your way through Beijing International or Shenzhen Bao'an Airport you will already spot many characteristics that differentiate China from the rest of the World.

I encourage you to read this book with an open mind and curiosity. China is an interesting and fascinating place with beautiful nature, mind-blowing skylines, and some of the most delicious cuisine in the World. With its now more than forty years of opening-up, China plays an increasingly important role in this world, which makes it even more important for people from all over the world to get a better understanding of Chinese culture and the role that China might play in the future.

Chinese businesses are expanding outside of the Mainland and Chinese food is conquering the world, following the many Chinese who are living abroad. All this might leave someone wondering if the success China is experiencing over the last decade and its steady growth are just thanks to the opening-up policy Deng Xiaoping promoted, or if there are some typical Chinese characteristics, that partly cause this success, too. With the many examples in this book, the deep-dive into China's long history, diverse present, and future the judgement about this is ultimately up to you.

I will try to keep this book interesting and enlightening. Therefore, I will not only present the current numbers and facts or walk you through the history step by step but instead diverge from the underlying academic research and tell the story about China in a hopefully interesting and engaging way. This will allow us to understand where China is coming from, how it used to work and which characteristics survived over the thousands of years. With all this knowledge at hand we will make, as promised, some predictions about China's future. In addition to describing the history and the current state, academic research and the combined knowledge of many great researchers from all over the world will help us to understand the different aspects in a greater context. I, for my part, will share with you my personal experience, anecdotes and comment on things that fascinated and impressed me.

# THE STRUCTURE OF THIS BOOK

This book is split into three parts, covering the past, the present, and the future of the People's Republic of China. Each part plays an important role in understanding China as a whole, with each part building on the previous.

In the beginning of this book we will take a step back and have a look into China's history and learn more about the many dynasties that ruled over this eastern empire. We will talk about innovation, developments, and trends that were and still are growing within China, concepts like Confucianism and Taoism and we will see how China transformed itself into a Communist country over time. From here we will look ahead of what will come and try to predict what will change and what will remain.

For all this, we will compress the knowledge of many books and thousands of years into just a few pages. So, if you want to get a deeper understanding of the history of China, the many wars and amazing stories about betrayal and assassinations, I encourage you to have a look into the bibliography and read more about the topics that interest you the most. In the beginning, I mentioned to you that China's past is as colourful as a rainbow and in my opinion extremely fascinating. Therefore, it will be unavoidable for us to only cover a small amount of the many facets that China has. I promise, though, it will be enough to build a foundation for what comes in the following two chapters. After China's past, we will have a look at China today. For this we will look at different aspects of the daily life of the Chinese people. We will see how different aspects and problems are dealt with in China and get a first understanding of the pragmatism that Deng Xiaoping praised. Furthermore, we will see, how the past is impacting the present. At this point it won't be hard for you to spot differences between China's approach and the way things are dealt with in the western World. In this part, we will also connect the dots between the past and the present and will jump back once in a while to expand on the knowledge we build in the first part.

I will keep the conclusion short, as the purpose of this book is to show you the differences between China and the West, rather than making bold predictions about what the future of China will be like. Nevertheless, we will have a look at trends, technologies, and characteristics that have emerged in the past and are still emerging in today's China and think about how they will impact the China of the future. Similar to the second part, in this part we will try to connect the present-day China with a possible future and draw conclusions out of emerging developments.

After all this, you are already a big step ahead of most people in better understanding China. Rather than having subjective views and making wild guesses you will have a good foundation of knowledge. The knowledge you will gain through this book will help you in shaping business relationships, building long-lasting friendships and appreciating China a little bit more rather than following uneducated comments about this country. You will definitely be well equipped enough to shine at the next dinner-talk about China and you should have no problems impressing the person sitting next to you.

In order to make reading the book an enjoyable experience, rather than a struggle, I decided to not use citation within the text. The key resources can be found at the end of this book.

I also want to apologise in advance at this point. Throughout the book I might be using the male form "he" rather than a gender-neutral "he/she". This is mainly due to old habit and my perception that "he/she" doesn't read well. With it I don't want to undermine the importance of women or worse see them as less relevant.

That being said, let's start.

# First Part

## The History of China

# WHERE IT ALL BEGAN

S imilar to Europe, China has a history that dates back hundreds of years and that has formed the character of its people and its government. When people think about China today, most people think about the post 1949 China in which the Communist Party of China (the CCP) was the ruling power, after it proclaimed the People's Republic of China on 1 October 1949. However, China's history reaches further back than 1949 and many ruling dynasties took part in forming the China that we know today.

In the introduction I mentioned that the history of China is as colourful as a rainbow. Now you will see for yourself what I mean by that and how colourful, interesting, and dramatic the history of China really was. Like many people, you might be biased, thinking that great inventions only come from Germany, the United Kingdom, the United States of America or other countries where famous universities drove innovation. You will see however, that China was almost always a leading player when it comes to innovation and development, with the West usually being the one trailing behind. Only the more recent industrial revolution gave an advantage to western countries. The industrial revolution allowed the European and American countries to undergo a great development, but the history of China might prove, that this head start will not last forever and that China will catch up sooner rather than later.

As the purpose of this book is to help you understand China better, we will not go all the way back to the first inhabitation of China more than 1 million years ago. Instead, we will start with one of China's earliest dynasties, the Shang Dynasty, which existed between 1600 – 1046 BC and work our way up to the present day. We will talk about conflicts, developments, innovations, and discuss important schools of thought like Buddhism, Confucianism, and Taoism at the end of this chapter. Afterwards, we will talk about the lessons that we can learn from China's history.

You can see the upcoming pages as a short summary of the history of China. To focus on the important parts of this history many conflicts and wars are kept short and many names of warlords and emperors are left out in order to put the focus on the events rather than the people. To get a better understanding of the conflicts and wars I encourage you to study the history of China in a greater depth. For now however, we will start our own journey through the history of China starting with the Shang dynasty.

# THE SHANG DYNASTY (1600 – 1028 BC)

嘗

W
e start off in a blur, as there is not a lot of information about the origin of the Shang dynasty available. Even less so about the Xia dynasty that came before that of the Shang, which is why we will not talk about it at this point. We do however know, that already back at the time of the Shang a sort of class-system existed. Alongside the Shanxi mountains (山西) and north of the yellow river (黄河) grew a new civilization. First settlements in the form of houses and simple agriculture farming started during the time of the Shang. The houses that the people of the Shang dynasty built had a rectangular style and can actually still be seen in parts of modern Chinese architecture.

It is interesting to notice that at this point in our timeline China is already suffering from a scarcity in metal. This characteristic will return over and over again throughout the history of China, as China was always suffering from a shortage of metals and insufficient production material throughout its long history and had to come up with ways to increase the supply of these metals. This made China dependent on trade and imports of many materials early on and might explain China's need for outwards movement and expansion.

Around 1300 BC, only a limited number of bronze vessels were available and the few that existed were mainly used for religious purposes. Another fascinating fact about this early China is that back then silk was already available, probably originating from the south of China. This shows that the great knowledge of silk making existed for a long time already.

Even a sort of wine existed back at the time of the Shang. Wine, probably produced from millet, used to be a popular drink more than 3300 years ago! This makes someone wonder, why even today the Chinese cannot compete with foreign wine production even though they had such a long time to figure out how to make good wine. Maybe it's my foreign palate, though, that has never really adopted to the sweet taste of Baiju (白酒).

Thankfully for the Shang, wine and liquor were not at the centre of the Shang dynasty and neither were the bronze vessels. The main focus was still on simple agricultural production for family use.

At the centre of the Shang dynasty was their king, with artisans following him in order. This meant that China managed to create a first class-system early on. Considering the point in time this is quite revolutionary! It seems fascinating that already such a long time ago the king had its own little bureaucratic machine, with officials, priest, scribes and military officials working for him.

Interestingly, the king gave his approximately three million citizens a lot of autonomy, too, and mainly functioned as a religious leader and supreme lord. This function helped him gather such a great number of people under his rule as religion became more and more important. Religious leadership is characteristic for an early success in civilisation as it (oftentimes for the first time) allows for big groups to gather and fight together in a magnitude that would not be possible without a religious centre. It is this development that provided the edge against family-oriented tribes who could oftentimes not manage groups bigger than a hundred people. As you will see, this is something, that is also characteristic for other upcoming dynasties where the emperor or king functioned in a similar religious position.

Managing a country of three million people is no easy task though and without a strong centre China's stability is hard to protect. Therefore, around 1028 BC a 260-days-long war against tribes in the south-east started and lead to instability in the country. This instability showed that while China was already united under one ruler the centre still had to be strengthened in order to protect China in times of chaos. Since a strong core was not present it was almost impossible to protect the Shang dynasty from its collapse. The empire collapsed and the 260 days long war marked the end of the Shang dynasty.

# THE ZHOU DYNASTY (1028 – 256 BC)

The Zhou dynasty begins where the Shang dynasty ended, in the year 1028 BC. This period is the first period that will have a strong impact on China as we know it today as this was a period where some of the first truly "Chinese" characteristics developed.

In contrast to the Shang, the Zhou dynasty emerged from the northwest around the Shaanxi area (陕西省), which is home to the famous and beautiful city of Xi'an. Xi'an will later find its glory by becoming the capital of the Qin, western Han, Sui, and Tang dynasties which we will talk more about in later parts of this book.

Before the Zhou dynasty was recognised for what it was, the Zhou and Shang lived next to each other. With an eastward migration of the Zhou, more and more of their original culture absorbed elements of the old Shang culture and both merged over time. While the one power (Shang) lost more and more of its importance and started to diminish, the other (Zhou) kept growing and found its glory.

With the growing power of the Zhou their leader, Wu Wang, decided to push into Honan, the former capital of the Shang dynasty to conquer the territory that was across the yellow river. Due to this strategic move a new "united" empire ruled by the Zhou emerged and with it started the actual history of China.

The first course of action of the new Zhou empire was to turn the country into a feudal state. The new territory that had to be governed by Wu Wang was enormous in size and as one can expect, the absence of emails, telephones, and other good communication platforms made ruling a difficult undertaking. Information had to be spread by foot and the paths were narrow and long. Thus, a feudal system turned out to be handy as it helped in governing and ruling over a large population that was spread all across what is now western China.

Most of the territorial rulers were also members of the Zhou ruling family or heads of allied tribes which helped to align interests. In theory the Zhou king ruled over the feudal lords and the allied tribes had their own sub-lords, which created a first step to the later established land ownership of families that shaped China in a unique way.

Fast forward to the year 500 BC around a thousand feudal states existed, oftentimes only consisting of a small size and region, with a local feudal lord ruling over a specific area. At this time most of the feudal lords established new cities as centres of their territory and laid the ground work for the still existing cities with their famous rectangular design and central crossroads that we see today.

What strikes me personally the most is how not only the city design still exist today, but that even more than 2500 years ago characteristics like resettlement of whole populations were similarly part of the Chinese culture as we observe in the present. These resettlements oftentimes took place to better govern the people and to improve their standard of living. The idea was simple: Create a planned urban area and fill it with skilled craftsmen and merchants from surrounding areas to keep the city alive and growing. It is therefore quite interesting that the word for merchant today is shāng rén (商人) or "Shang" person if you would like to translate it, indicating that many of the former Shang ended up working as merchants in the new cities. That is of course if they did not end up as a farmer or a labourer. Of course, we should not generalize at this point because the current situation of resettlement in China is more complex. The underlying idea is similar though; improve the standard of living by creating economic centres that can create spill over effects, help in governing the population, and most importantly help in the transition from agricultural to factory focused work.

Next to the cities villages existed which showed their dependency and gratitude by sending gifts and grain to the lords in the cities. This later translates into a formal tax system.

With the Zhou came not only a patriarchate family system but also the worship of heaven, which probably derived from the Turkish people and found its way to China. In addition to that, the Zhou introduced and spread the idea of ancestor-worship, a variation of this is still part of the Chinese culture today. The idea back then was that next to the life-soul (the part that dies with us) a personality-soul existed that lives as long as someone is remembered. This kind of ancestor worship can also be found in Southeast Asia where it is still practiced today in some regions. Later on, the concept of heaven-worship found its way into the family system and as the two merged the family ruler was declared as the "son of heaven".

While the intention of the feudal system was to help govern the wide territory and its millions of people it later turned out to be the root of some trouble. With the introduction of the feudal system, the ruling house of the Zhou dynasty lost more and more of its own power over the years since ruling over such a large empire still represented a huge challenge for many leaders. In addition to that, many of the feudal lords were busy fighting their own battles and ruling over their people and thus showed little interest for the powers far away that were having little impact on their daily life.

Adding to this was pressure from the neighbours of the Zhou empire. The Turks and Mongols who still mainly lived a nomadic lifestyle, enjoyed easy access to agricultural products by raiding the settlements of Zhou farmers. This nomad culture still characterizes Mongolia in the coming years and their dependency on raiding Chinese farmland drove them into a difficult position later on in history.

What is still important to notice is that at this point in history a first form of a common Chinese language emerged as even the ruling class adapted to the general vocabulary of the people.

Having a united language is important for the development of a nation and the identification with it. Nevertheless, the Chinese population was still split into two parts, with the ruling classes in the cities and the lower classes outside the cities on the farms or in segregated parts of the cities.

In 771 BC a new conflict erupted for the Zhou empire as they were attacked from the north. The current ruler of the Zhou empire was killed in a battle and the early centre of their power, Shaanxi (陕西), was lost to the enemy. The Zhou had to escape to the south which led to the forced growth of their second capital, Luoyang (洛阳市) under the rule of the former prince. Luoyang, a city worth visiting, creatively earned its name for being on the sunny ("yang") side of the Luo River.

The former prince and new king had a difficult situation to face and was in a dilemma as he owed his survival to his feudal lords and was indebted to them, but at the same time also lost most of his power and ability to pay back the debt. This led to the later development that he lost most of his decision-making power and became a sanctified ruler and - with most of his original power lost - nothing more but a symbol of former glory. He was lucky though, as his role as son of heaven, and thus ruler of the world, still made him indispensable. At least for the time being.

While the king was following his new found duties as son of heaven in his new capital Luoyang, the development of the originally feudal towns into feudal states did not stop. It became custom to unite and follow the strongest feudal lord rather than the Zhou king and while the Zhou empire still existed, the power did not lie in the same hands anymore.

Many powerful feudal lords entered the scene. One of them was the feudal lord of the state of Qi who grew to new power after the devastating attack from the north took place. His state developed into the main centre of the most developed civilization at that time, with a strong focus on trade and the revolutionary use of money. The Qi ruled over what is now known as Shandong (山东省), a coastal province in western China. But the rule of the Qi was short, as no single ruler and feudal state could exercise the control over all other states and unite the control.

One of the most important modern artefacts of the Zhou dynasty is their intellectual influence on today's China. Between 550 and 280 BC the major fundamental influence for Chinese famous social order and its intellectual life emerged. After the Zhou king lost most of its power, it was not only time for the feudal lords to emerge, but also for the scholars and the former priests who gained a growing influence on the social life and traditions of the people.

Confucius, probably the best known and most famous of these new scholars, was born in 551 BC and it was finally his time to shine. However, for now, we will continue with the general history as the life of Confucius was quite usual and similar to that of many scholars of his time. As a matter of fact, Confucius did not come up with many revolutionary ideas, instead he mainly taught what every over scholar was teaching. But he should get at least some credit. He managed to systemize the existing ideas and to teach them to the right people so that his teachings were later written down. We will later come back to the ideas and teachings of Confucius and discuss them in more detail separately from this timeline of China's history.

It took a long time after that until Lao Tzu found the school of Taoism - another school of thought. In his work he tried to argue how man can live in harmony with the law of the universe.

In contrast to Confucius, who focused on how people should behave in their social environments, Lao Tzu tried to argue that mankind should not participate in the rites and ceremonies but should rather choose a self-imposed isolation. In a sense, Taoism is about passive achievement and individualistic anarchy. Lao Tzu believed, that if there was no active government everyone would be happy. It followed, that most of the Taoist moved outside of the cities and lived on farms, while the Confucianist gained more power in the cities. We will come back to Taoism later, and similar to Confucianism, discuss it separately from the general history of China.

Between 481 and 256 BC started what will turn out to be the end of the feudal system in China as we know it. This is a special period in which the existing structure of China and its many feudal states changed drastically. Since the Zhou king had little power left and almost no important function anymore, many of the feudal states gave up their allegiance to the Zhou king and saw themselves as independent. At this point in time a united China and a Chinese state as such was far from being realized.

As none of the independent feudal states had enough power or control to strive on its own - not even that of the Qi - alliances were formed to create new promising trade routes and growing prosperity for the citizens and feudal lords. As there was no strong centre to guide China, or whatever was left of the Zhou empire, the country was faced with turmoil and instability. Many of the alliances broke, new alliances were formed and the process repeated itself over and over again until many of the feudal lords were left with less than what they had before. In addition to this, a lot of the previously occupied land became free and many previously poor people started owning their own land. However, with the consistently increasing population, land became rare again and old traditions like giving new land to the youngest son could not always be followed.

It happened that during this time merchants started collecting formal taxes, too, as it became more and more difficult for the feudal lords to do so. This simple move helped the merchants to rise in their ranks and become the first administrative officials in the provinces of China.

As for many empires and countries at this time, the growth of the cities led to a higher demand of food, which consequently led to a necessary improvement in the infrastructure in form of roads and better-established transportation networks. In addition to this, the existing rivers grew in importance as they, too, helped transport food and materials to far away destinations. Even first canals were built as an early answer to the needed improvement in trade and transportation networks. At this point in time it is hard to turn away from the many small "revolutions" going on in China and it won't be the last time for us to see developments like these.

It is also quite remarkable to see how important money became in the day to day life for Chinese citizens. This new wealth helped many of the cities to develop into places of luxury and business. Even land could now be bought for money, a development that was unimaginable in the past.

An important school of thought that grew to importance at the end of the Zhou dynasty was the school of the "Legalist". The Legalist saw a decrease in the old powers of the feudal lords and saw the ruler and his chancellor as the leading figure and everyone else as either poor or rich citizens. They saw it to be the responsibility of the chancellor to draft laws and to make crucial decision affecting the county. The ruler on the other hand had again little to say and should not intervene with the government as he was still only seen as a representative figure. Here again, we will come back to the Legalist school later in this book and learn more about it.

The Zhou dynasty is the longest dynasty in Chinese history and it built a strong foundation for the many dynasties that followed. The Zhou introduced money, a united language, and leading schools of thought, just to mention a few. Despite all this, the Zhou dynasty showed first indications of an upcoming ending around 300 BC when the first feudal system finally broke up.

Around 256 BC the most drastic changes happened as the last ruler of the Zhou dynasty stepped down in favor of the feudal lord of the Qin. This event marks the ending of the Zhou dynasty.

It is hard to ignore how the Zhou empire could never really recover from a previous loss of its north-western territory and how the only remaining representative function of the emperor let to the final decline of the Zhou dynasty as he failed to unite the people underneath him. China proved to be weakened again without a strong centre. The Zhou empire started in a spectacular way but it came to an end nevertheless.

# THE QIN DYNASTY (256 – 207 BC)

We reached the year 256 BC, the official beginning of the Qin, one of the better-known dynasties in China's history.

The territory is still the same as that of the last Zhou emperor (not really surprising) and reaches from Shaanxi (陕西) to Gansu (甘肃). To the north China still faces an uncultivatable desert that stops expansion to the north. To the south, unpassable mountains create a similar obstacle for China.

Already before 256 BC the Qin made a good amount of money trading with neighbouring countries like Turkistan and over the years trade in general became an important factor in the daily lives of many people. For the other parts of China, the province of the Qin was actually seen as a barbarian state because the Qin decided to abandon the feudal system early on, going against conviction[1]. Nevertheless, the Qin state was by far economically the strongest state in the eastern world and in a way revolutionary for abandoning the feudal system.

The Qin dynasty was strongly influenced by the Legalist school of thought and had a consequently strong bureaucratic structure, which still remained an important part of the Qin empire even after they abandoned their feudal system.

Fast forward ten years, to around 247 BC, a former merchant managed to reach the highest ranks and become the head of the state of the Qin. This, as unspectacular as it might seem written down in text, is illustrating a drastic and important change in China at the time.

The former merchant and new ruler was the famous Qin Shi Huang (秦始皇)[2]. Qin Shi Huang is probably best known today for the terracotta army that was built close to his tomb just outside of Xi'an to protect him in his afterlife. In addition to that, he is also known for his unification of the many diverse states behind a single Great Wall of China. In fact, both of these magnificent relicts of the Qin dynasty are still on the list of highlights of many visitors to China these days.

What Qin Shi Huang is probably less known for is his work on a massive new road system. This system was equally important to the development of the Qin state as the Great Wall was for its protection. If you have the chance to visit China, I recommend visiting the Great Wall or terracotta army rather than checking out some old road systems, though.

The above-mentioned Great Wall of China was constructed around 214 BC out of a system of many single frontiers in order to protect the empire from increasing number of attacks from the north. Remember, in the south were still the mountains, which functioned as a great

---

[1] I personally find this very characteristic even for modern times, as people easily judge that whatever is different to them to be wrong and believe that their way of thinking is the right way.

[2] Quite funny but maybe not surprising is that the name of the first emperor of the Qin translates to "First emperor of the Qin". Of course, he was not born with this name, his birth name was either Ying Zheng (嬴政) or Zhao Zheng (趙政).

natural fortress. In the north however, the Qin dynasty had to face open land and robbing nomad tribes. A construction of a big connected wall in the north was thus the consequential action to protect the citizen of the Qin empire.

With the new ruler - a follower of the Legalist school - more and more supporters of the Legalist school rose to power, taking important positions in the state. With the new advisors in place the power of the Qin grew fast and between 230 to 222 BC the remaining feudal states had almost no other chance than to come under the rule of the Qin, too.

This final and important unification of "China" marks the beginning of the imperial era of China and is a critical milestone in the history of China. It stands out again at this point in history, China is at its best when it has a strong centre. It is this strong core that provides the necessary stability for economic, social, and scientific development.

During the time of unification, the formal feudal lords were deprived of their power and instead a uniform system of administration was set-up – just the way the Legalist like it. In addition to this, military officials were given less power and at the head of each province was not only a military governor, but also a civil governor and a third controlling official. This system prevented the creation of new feudal lords[3].

With the unification of the feudal states came a corresponding further unification of the language that followed the earlier examples of the Zhou dynasty. One measure to unify the language was to publish a first list of official words. This was a crucial development needed in order to bring the many states that diverted over the years back together. Furthermore, weights and measures were unified, too, showing again how influential the Qin dynasty was for the development of an overall united China.

Qin Shi Huang, the first emperor, fell sick on one of his travels and died in 210 BC. While he called himself the first emperor of the Qin, there was never a second. The death of the emperor led a disastrous

---

[3] This system is similar to the later existing Chinese administration.

rebellion and a quick change in power. As a consequence, the Han dynasty emerged at 206 BC after many years of turmoil. The Han would have more luck maintaining their power and would remain the ruling dynasty for the next 400 years to come.

## THE HAN DYNASTY (206 BC – 220 AD)

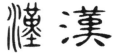

The beginning of the Han dynasty can be seen as the beginning of the Chinese middle age. While the Han dynasty lasted for around 400 years, it was actually temporarily interrupted by the short-lived Xin dynasty (9 – 23 AD); which is why today the Han dynasty is split into two periods: The period of the western Han from 206 BC – 9 AD and the period of the eastern Han from 25 – 220 AD.

Today, the majority of Chinese see themselves as "Han"[4] and even the Chinese characters that are used today are referred to as "Han characters" indicating that most of them have their roots in the Han dynasty.

One major attribute of the Han was the revival of the so far quite absent Confucianism school. This revival happened around 141 BC when Confucianism was practiced in the government again. Consequently, it also found its way into the legal system and the court and took over where the Legalist school was previously dominating. This "reborn" Confucianism would remain of importance until the fall of the Qing dynasty around 1911 AD. Thus, Confucianism influenced

---

[4] The word hàn rén (汉人) translates to "Chinese person" up until today.

China for more than 2000 years. This is one of the reasons why Confucianism still plays such an important role in today's China and why it is so important for us to understand if we want to understand China. It shaped the Chinese society and left a permanent mark in the way things are dealt with and since it is such an important component of China's history, we will talk about it separately at the end of the first part.

With the Han dynasty came another wave of economic growth and the former Zhou-introduced money economy found more and more followers during the time of the Han. In fact, it grew consistently making it one of the major drivers of trade and economic growth in the region and an important component to the success of the Han dynasty. One of the other drivers of economic growth was the increase in trade with foreign countries and the establishment of the famous Silk Road[5]. This was very different to the previous decades before. The Silk Road itself was a connection of trade routes that helped to connect the eastern and the western world and grew to a huge trade network over the decades. Up until today it still remains of utmost importance for Chinese trade and still cast its shadow above modern projects like the Belt and Road Initiative (BRI). We will talk more about the Belt and Road Initiative in the last part of this book as it will play a crucial role in the future of China.

Despite all the economic growth, the period of the Han dynasty was not only marked with trade growth and prosperity. During the rule of the Han, many military campaigns took place, one of them against the northern enemies. Additionally, the conquering of the western part of Korea in 108 BC took place during the time of the Han dynasty. Visitors of both countries can easily spot the similarities that exist between China and Korea up until today. Not only the writing system of both countries but also aspects like architecture, food, and culture still overlaps in both countries.

---

[5] Who would have thought, that the name of the Silk Road derives from the lucrative trade in silk? If you remember, the Chinese were acquainted to working with silk already since the Shang dynasty and masters in silk production.

Despite the effort to bring new prosperity to the country through conquering, like it was the case in previous dynasties, the wars that were carried out by the different Han emperors turned out to be ruinous for the country itself. The ruling powers of the Han underestimated the cost of maintaining a large army and the difficulty of a necessary continuous occupation of their newly won regions. A mistake China will do again many times during other dynasties.

In the end, even peasants had to enrol for the military service and whoever was spared joining the army, was faced with higher taxes to feed the many hungry mouths. To overcome the increasing poverty, the government decided to increase controls over its citizen and at the same time implemented more and more state-owned monopolies. A form of these early state-owned enterprise (SOE) still exists in China today and the development of these so called SOEs will also play an important role for China's future and economic strength.

Shortly after these events took place, the Han period was set on pause and the short rule of the Xin dynasty began. Wang Mang, who first ruled in the background a few years by placing his kids on the throne, finally declared that heaven actually commanded him to rule over the country rather than his children.

During this brief interruption of the Han dynasty from 9 – 25 AD the short-lived Xin dynasty took over power, but could not maintain it and lost it due to increasing instability and chaos almost as fast as it gained it. However, at this point in time almost all members of the former imperial family were removed as a precautious measure.

Wang Mang managed to maintain his power for a few years using propaganda and a strict ruling hand. Following this was a growing unrest amongst the people. The people were increasingly unsatisfied with their leader and in the end his ruling was brought to an end after turmoil took over the country. Wang Mang was killed in his throne room in 22 AD. He could not create a centre strong enough to maintain his power.

However, while Wang Mang was dead, no end of the riots were in sight and no new leader was emerging out of the uprising. China was like many times before, covered with turmoil and chaos. Only in 25 AD, three years and many deaths later emerged a new emperor, starting the period of the so called "eastern Han".

The long and deadly fights also had something good, if you would want to say so. Due to the many years of fighting, chaos, and struggle the population reduced up to a point that made it possible for almost everyone to own their own land again. Similar to previous periods we can see how the population/land-owning ratio balanced again thanks to the chaos in the country. In addition to that, many of the former peasant and slaves ended up free of debt and free from their former owners as their lords and money lenders in the cities were no longer alive or were too occupied trying to stay alive.

After the war was over, the Han started rebuilding their economy again and grew fast early on. They again improved their economic condition, which helped them to recover from the years of the uprising.

This economic improvement continued for a few years until around 80 AD. In the year 80 AD, despite the increasing trade with foreign countries, the political situation within China started to slowly worsen again. This time the political instability originated from another source, though - the eunuchs[6].

The increase in wealth and prosperity among the Han emperors allowed them to have more wives and concubines than every other emperor before them. However, this "luxury" if you would want to call it this way also asked for a bigger number of eunuchs, who were in charge of managing everything. An army of eunuchs to be precise.

The eunuchs served the emperor in his chambers and thus, it is not to surprising that they also formed an important political factor - they were able to influence the emperor in his decision making. And influencing the emperor they did.

---

[6] Eunuchs were castrated men and served the emperor as his personal slaves. Due to their castration they were seen as very loyal since they were neither able to seduce women nor to father children who could enthrone the emperor.

Political upheaval started again. First slow but it progressed over the years and by 184 AD a political rebellion crystalized into the so called "Yellow Turban Rebellion".

In the turmoil that followed this rebellion, three states within the former Han region tried to gain predominant power over all of China. None of the states could win the control though and the chaos that came out of the wars lasted for many years. Only around 220 AD, after many years of fighting, did the Han dynasty came to an end. As none of the states could gain predominant power over the others the way for the first division within China was opened. This division is known as the time of the "Three Kingdoms".

In the end, the Han Period was that of the final completion and consolidation of the social order and a period of a reintroduction of Confucianism. The following period was one with new conflicts and new partition.

# THE THREE KINGDOMS (220 – 265 AD)

三 国

By the year 220 AD the period of the Han was over and the former unified kingdom was again divided into several kingdoms, each with its own dynasty going forward. China will be divided for many centuries now and only in 580 AD will China be reunited again.

By the time the Han dynasty ended, the Wei dynasty began first, but almost immediately two other army commanders declared themselves as emperor and thus split the country in three parts. The three kingdoms during the period from 220 until 265 AD were Wei (魏), Shu (蜀), and Wu (吴). The Wei ruling in the north and Shu and Wu ruling in the south-west and south-east, respectively.

The capitals of all three Kingdoms are still well-known cities within China. Chengdu (成都市), the famous "Panda-City" in the Sichuan province is not only a great city to visit if you like pandas or spicy food but was also the former capital of the Shu dynasty. The capital of the Wei was in Luoyang (洛阳市), the former capital of the Zhou dynasty. Luoyang will be an important city for many more dynasties to come. The capital(s) of the Wu dynasty were Wuchang and Jianye. Up until today the name "Wuchang" remains in common use for the part of urban Wuhan (武汉市), the capital of Hubei province and the most populous city in central China. Jianye is now one of the eleven districts in Nanjing (南京市), the capital of the Jiangsu province. This shows us that while many things change, long existing cities usually grow and remain important over time because they provide a necessary foundation for growth and future development and thus offer a crucial advantage over new cities.

With the division of China came the growth of Buddhism, which previously played only a little or rather close to no role in the lives of many Chinese. As you can guess, we will talk more about Buddhism at the end of the first part of this book, too. With Buddhism, which originated from India, also came the growing knowledge within China of the many countries west of it that were not barbarian states as thought, but almost equally developed countries. This made the former belief, that the emperor was the son of heaven no longer defendable as the emperor only had power in China and not in the rest of the word. Consequently, with old believes gone, new ideas and thoughts found their way into the minds of the Chinese over the decade. One of them being the above-mentioned school of Buddhism.

Not only did the horizon of the Chinese grew, but also their spectrum of food grew and former wheat cultures were substituted with new rice cultures growing in their wet fields. Rice will later help to feed the population and contributed a lot to the immense population growth in China.

The period of the three kingdoms was mainly marked with rivalry between the three. This rivalry consumed most of the attention and resources which makes it no surprise that only little innovation and development took place during the period of the three kingdoms. This rivalry actually went on over the entire existents of the three kingdoms.

As we have learned, a weak centre oftentimes comes with an unpromising outlook for China.

During the year 265 AD the dynasty in the north changed from Wei to Jin, which marks a point in time in which a new important dynasty began. This is why we count the period from 265 until 420 AD as the period of the Jin dynasty. The Jin will last for another century and leave, like other dynasties before, their impact on China, too.

# THE JIN DYNASTY (265 – 420 AD)

Similar to the Han dynasty, the Jin dynasty is also split into two periods. The first being the period of the western Jin and the second being the period of the eastern Jin. The era of the western Jin lasted from 265 until 316 AD while that of the eastern Jin lasted from 317 until 420 AD.

Before diving into the Jin dynasty we should have a quick look back to the Han dynasty. What I did not mention in the previous section, and should probably mention now, is that the Wei empire actually managed to overthrow the Shu dynasty and rule over their territory at the end of the period of the three kingdoms. This means that once the Jin dynasty took over the Wei dynasty they were actually ruling over the territory of the Wei and Shu, which only left the Wu in the southeast as an independent empire.

With the Wei changing to Jin in the year 265 AD a new dynasty began. Soon after that, the newly formed Jin dynasty conquered the remaining southern Wu dynasty in 280 AD and with that the former empire almost reached it previous glory.

Unfortunately, the period of unification was short. After a devastating war the western Jin experienced an uprising of the nomadic people. Also, the subsequent eastern Jin (317 until 420 AD) were plagued with militaristic authorities and crises later on, which seems to be a trend throughout the entire Jin dynasty.

During the uprising of the western Jin dynasty, civil war started and the just recently reunited China lost control of its northern territory. That means, that China was now split up again into new self-proclaimed states. This period, which took place around 304 AD is also known as the era of the "Sixteen Kingdoms". Nevertheless, for simplicity reasons we still count this episode as a chapter of the Jin dynasty as no other dominating power emerged during this time.

With the uprising and chaos, the north unfortunately lost many of its cultural achievements and its aristocracy. Up until the Jin dynasty this had been the main social class that maintained and kept alive Confucianism in the northern part of China.

Interestingly, we can observe that Confucianism is always closely linked to the upper and ruling classes rather than to the peasants. The peasants instead showed more interest in Buddhism and Taoism.

We will later see how the former nobility will grow again and how it will play an important part in the history of China. For now, we will continue with the history of China.

Around 317 AD the eastern Jin ruled over the little remaining territory in the east of the country. At this point in time the Jin already lost most of their former glory and power. Despite all that they managed to stick around for another 100 years before another dynasty took over.

Since much of the previously existing Confucianism thought disappeared in the north together with the gentry, there was newly created room for other believes. Buddhism which came from India to China during the Han dynasty profited from this empty space and experienced a new growth due to the many existing and growing number of peasants and people in the north. Furthermore, Buddhism also found its acceptance in the ranks of the ruling class as the ruling class started to like the idea of telling the poor - who had to suffer hardship and injustice – that they would be reborn into high ranks, having a better life in their next life rather than now[7].

Today, it is generally accepted that it was around the time of the Jin dynasty that the Chinese country population first identified themselves as Chinese, too. Thus, the efforts of the previous dynasties started to pay off.

With all these changes taking place there was no rest in sight and the again separated kingdom saw clashes between the different states. This continuous fighting finally lead to a second and final division of the Jin dynasty and the era of the eastern Jin ended, too, when their kingdom was overthrown in a brutal battle.

---

[7] Who would have thought this? Merchants favoured Buddhism, too, as they took advantage of Buddhist monasteries and used them as banks and warehouses early on during the dynasty and would continue to do so for many decades. These Buddhist merchants will play an important role in the development of China and innovations like paper money.

# THE SOUTHERN AND NORTHERN DYNASTIES
## (420 – 589 AD)

# 南北朝

F ollowing the collapse of the last Jin dynasty and the "Sixteen Kingdoms" came the time of the of the so-called southern and northern dynasties.

During the time of the southern and northern dynasties, Buddhism[8] kept spreading further trough the country and in addition to technological advancement, arts and culture also found new soil to grow. In addition to the growth of Buddhism, culture and arts, China also underwent a new era of growth in the old philosophical tradition of Taoism. Contrary to Confucianism, which mainly focused on how people should behave, Taoism focused on following the law of the universe and a self-imposed isolation.

As the name of the dynasty suggest, China was split into two main areas. The area in the north was ruled by the so-called northern Wei from 386 until 535 AD. After the year 535 AD, the north was split even further into eastern and western Wei and thereafter into northern Qi and Zhou. This is not to be confused with the previous dynasties of Wei and Zhou.

During the early days the new emperor in the north appointed a Buddhist monk as head of a new state church and gave him important rights like using slaves to build temples, which helped to further strengthened the position of Buddhism in early China. Since the Chinese Buddhist monks profited a lot from the emperors' decisions, they agreed that they will bow to the emperor and subsequently regarded him as the reincarnation of Buddha. This is a huge step,

---

[8] The special form of Buddhism that spread during this time was called Mahayana Buddhism.

making the emperor almost a God. This is especially remarkable considering that Buddhism did not originate from China itself but came from its Indian neighbour originally. Despite this development and the growing importance of Buddhism, Confucianism managed to slowly take back its position as the main state religion during the end of the northern and southern dynasties as it still offered many advantages to the gentry. Over time, the strong segregation between Buddhism and Confucianism would disappear and both schools would exist next to each other and merge more and more together.

For now, let's have a look at the south, though. Here we find a comparable huge population of Han people, that managed to survive the military attacks from the northern nomadic tribes and subsequently emigrated to the south to find protection, peace, and a new home. This allowed the south to grow not only in size but also economically compared to earlier years.

However, in his book "Buddhism in Chinese History", Arthur F. Wright points out correctly that "when we speak of the area of the Yangtze valley and below in the period of disunion, we must banish from our minds the picture of the densely populated, intensively cultivated South China of recent centuries." The pictures of the Pearl River Delta and its enormous cities that some people might have in their heads is still far from becoming realized. For this we have to wait a few more hundred years. This is still the beginning of China and for now deadly mosquitoes and missing trade routes still make it hard and unattractive to go too far south.

The south also didn't accept the spread of Buddhism as easy as the north and many debated if Buddhism should be allowed its place next to the wide spread Confucianism. However, similar to the north it was too late already to stop the spread of Buddhism in the south. In the end both, the Taoist and the Buddhist found their place next to Confucianist and became more tolerant of each other, which lead to an overall more diverse China at the time.

# THE SUI DYNASTY (581 – 618 AD)

# 隋朝

In 580 the last of the northern dynasties ended and the Sui dynasty managed to achieve what seemed to be impossible for almost four centuries. Under the rule of the Sui dynasty China went from a politically fragmented nation to a reunited country after the last autonomous dynasty surrendered to the Sui in 589 AD. This is an important milestone in the history of China as it marks the end of a divided China.

The new united China, as we will see during the periods of the Tang, Song, Ming, and Qing was stronger and more impactful than the many separated states that existed until this point. A united China is in a sense like a strong and resilient rope that consist of many thin and fragile pieces. Each piece alone might not be strong enough, but together they build a powerful and durable tool.

To understand the Sui better you should know that the newly matured Sui dynasty was actually founded by a Han person from the south. Equally important to know is that the freshly reunited China achieved a critical victory of the gentry over the remaining warrior nomads from the north which put many southern Han in a better position. Also, culturally many changes were introduced to the recently reunited China and many foreign characteristics like music and clothing were adopted by growing parts of the Chinese population.

Despite, or rather due to the drastic changes in China, the Sui dynasty was faced with many difficulties during its short period of reign. Reuniting China was a task that no one manage to bear for the last centuries and the long separation of the different regions left its mark on the country. The long separation of the north and the south lead to many differences between both parts ranging from population size, culture, language, all the way to economic structures. Reuniting these very different states seemed like merging largely different neighboring countries like Germany and the Netherlands. It would be possible but tonnes of work would be needed in order to achieve a harmonic union.

During the reign of the Sui dynasty the capital moved back to its old home Luoyang (洛阳市), the former capital of the Zhou dynasty, close to or let's rather say on the sunny side of the Luo river. Moving the capital back to Luoyang had many advantages as the location of the city was beneficial in protecting the country and many old structures still remained which made it easy to use the city for administrative work and as a useful decision-making base.

While the Sui introduced imperial exams to recruit officials for their administrative work in the city the Sui dynasty is mostly known for other things. An achievement of the Sui dynasty includes the construction of the great canals, which was aimed at facilitating the transportation of grain and other resources from regions in the south back to the new (old) capital in the north. However, the construction of the great canals, including the world-famous "Grand Canal", overstrained the resources due to its enormous size and high cost. Nonetheless, the construction of the "Grand Canal" was an enormous achievement and a gigantic engineering project, especially considering the time, connecting the Yellow River (黄河) with the Yangtze river (长江). The "Grand Canal" which is also known as the Jing–Hang Grand Canal (京杭大运) is connecting Beijing and Hangzhou and not only the oldest but also the longest canal in the world[9] - a title that the Grand Canal still holds to this day.

While looking back at the achievement of building the "Grand Canal" is a great thing to do now, it was one of the reasons why the Sui dynasty failed in the end. The extreme over-expenditure on the canals – which unfortunately did not pay back during the period of the Sui – paired with an increasing extravagance of the ruler and additional warfare with the Turks in the west and the Koreans in the east lead to an

---

[9] The Grand Canal reaches a total length of 1,776 kilometres or 1,104 miles!

unspectacular end of the Sui dynasty which in the end could not maintain its never-ending expenses anymore. After the beginning of a dispute and unrest in the country the emperor tried to escape the growing unrest by moving further to the south. In the end however, all his efforts were for nothing as he was assassinated in the year 618 AD - ending the Sui dynasty once and for all.

# THE TANG DYNASTY (618 – 907 AD)

# 唐朝

The change from Sui to Tang dynasty did not go smoothly and for a while China was split up again into multiple states, that were fighting with each other. However, only five years later - in 623 AD –China was again reunited under one ruler. With the Tang dynasty began a new era of newfound prosperity that was about to last until 907 AD. The lessons from previous chapters, that China is strongest when it has a strong centre holds again and the Tang dynasty is a good example of this.

Additionally, the Tang period is another great example to show how advanced China was and how many steps ahead it was compared to the western pre-industrial-revolution world. During the period of the Tang a state secretariat was set up that was in charge of economics and political affairs as well as the financial affairs of the state. In Europe a similar system was not implemented until the eighteenth century!

One reason for the well organized and structured system of early China was the general need for a functioning administration. One reason for this is of course the huge population that needed to be governed, another being the enormous area of land that belong to China. It is estimated that during the Tang Period around fifty million people lived in China and the "new" capital of the Tang dynasty, Chang'an (today known as Xi'an), accounted for around two million people alone, making it the most populated city in the world at the time. The capital was filled with a huge number of officials to meet the administrative needs and many more people who came to Chang'an to find a better future for themselves and their children.

Over the years trade started to take off even further and more and more foreigners streamed into the east-Asian country to sell their exotic goods and in return brought home what was exotic to them. The Silk Road soon found a maritime partner with ships going all the way from the South China Sea to far away countries and empires in the west like the Abbasid Caliphate[10]. While the whole country was covered by the travelling merchants, a commercial network grew and the Silk Road developed even further into one of the most important trade routes in the world. Some foreigners settled in China, others travelled back home on the long routes along the Silk Road, and again others found their home in places along the Silk Road somewhere in-between China and the west.

Quite interesting is that while Confucianism was still the predominant belief and deeply rooted in the minds of the people, it was no longer actively discussed. Rather, Confucianism was seen as a general basis of morality. This again left new room for Buddhism to gradually grow and to become the predominant philosophical belief and religion next to Confucianism. Buddhism, which already coexisted next to Confucianism for a while, would soon be strongly connected with it.

The Tang dynasty ended abruptly in 690 AD with the death of its leader. The dead emperor was replaced by empress Wu – the first female leader – who made herself empress of yet another Zhou dynasty.

---

[10] This expansion completes the Silk Road as we know it with its land and water ways that built the foundation for the recent Belt and Road Initiative.

This dynasty didn't last too long however and in 705 AD - after this short interruption - the Tang dynasty was restored again. The Tang dynasty reached its peak shortly after this temporary disturbance during the reign of Emperor Tang Xuanzong (唐玄宗). Economic inflation was stable and even the death penalty was abolished in the year 747 AD, which is just another example for the progressive change that took place. During the time of the Tang a new land law was introduced which was aimed at spreading the ownership of land more equally but in the end, it failed to do so. Consequently, around the year 780 AD the law was finally abolished again and all that remained was a classification of the citizens into different castes.

Despite the increasing activities along the Silk Road, towards the end of the Tang dynasty trade steadily diminished. Additionally, multiple wrong decisions like the abolishment of the equal field system that was mentioned above lowered the inflow of new taxes which caused the state revenues to decline significantly. The official decline of the Tang dynasty began in 860 AD, which was caused by famine and a naturally following rebellion of the people. This was however closely linked and caused by the bad economic situation that emerged at the end of the Tang dynasty.

Many more rebellions started over the years and in addition to the already poor economic situation, the situation worsened when foreign warlords attacked the country to profit from China's weakness. In 879 AD most of the 200 thousand inhabitants of Guangzhou (广州) – the now thriving city in the Pearl River Delta – were killed by the hands of a vicious warlord. The same warlord who killed most of Guangzhou in 879 AD, Huang Chao, also managed to occupy the eastern capital Luoyang in 880 AD and ultimately conquered the well protected Chang'an in 881 AD. As you can guess - the time of the Tang to step down from the stage has come.

By the time Huang Chao was ultimately defeated by the remaining forces of the Tang army, there was nothing much left to save. The dynasty fell into a deep hole of political chaos and instability. This chaos and instability caused the final downfall and the end of the Tang dynasty. Wrong decisions like the abolishment of the equal field system which was one of the reasons for the lower tax inflow, as well the dependency on foreigners and foreign trade along the Silk Road were just some of the reasons for the downfall of this empire.

# THE FIVE DYNASTIES (907 – 960 AD)

## 五代

In 907 AD we saw another dynasty ending through an assassination and a period of transition in which China was again covered with turmoil and relative instability. It seems like history is repeating itself so the "new" division of China that we will cover here might not seem too surprising to you at this point.

The early post-Tang China was still affected by the rebellion that Huang Chao led and throughout the upcoming years five dynasties would emerge and take control over the old imperial heartland. An additional ten dynasties took control over areas in the south and the west. The ten dynasties in the south and west were mainly ruled by former military governors but were seen as illegitimate and are thus not given much credit. While they play their role in the history of China, we will not cover much of them as they are not of much importance to the future development of China. The five dynasties in the north were the Later Liang (907 – 923 AD), the Later Tang (923 – 936 AD), Later Jin (936 – 947 AD), Later Han (947 – 951 AD) and surprisingly another "Later" dynasty, the Later Zhou (951 – 960 AD).

While the south might have been seen as illegitimate, it was far better off than the north, as it still had a growing economy and prospering trade thanks to the local production of tea and porcelain – both products that were sold within the country and overseas since the early Tang dynasty. Porcelain played an especially important role for the export market ever since the Tang dynasty and its smooth and almost glass-like surface was wanted all over the world. No other country was able to create porcelain of such a beauty and quality at this point in history.

One of the things I find especially interesting about the period of the five dynasties is that it was also around this time that China first introduced paper money. The previously introduced money was mainly based on copper and other metals up until this point. This doesn't sound too special at first, but getting rid of copper and iron money had many advantages as the new paper money was easier to transport due to its light weight. A probably bigger advantage is that the government could now "print" money way easier whenever they wanted and actively participate in setting an inflation rate. The name of the new fiat money was Jiaozi (交子).

It probably isn't too big of a surprise to you that China also invented paper production earlier in its history, which made it even easier for China to switch to the production of paper money. Around the time of the Han dynasty the Chinese started to use paper for the first time and kept improving the papermaking process. By the time we reached the Tang dynasty papermills existed and paper became a cheaper, lighter, and more convenient material than its competitors.

The story of the invention of paper money goes like this: In the beginning merchants were still paying with copper money but the administration of it was difficult and costly and it was hard to control the amount in circulation since obviously copper was needed in order to create new money. This subsequently let to the fact that some provinces started to forbid the export of copper money out of their territory to control the amount of money – crazy right? Of course, the merchants weren't too happy about this as trade with foreign territories became quite difficult.

As a solution, deposit certificates were created to transfer the ownership of the copper based on the certificate that was issued earlier rather than the actual copper. It was these certificates that were then traded and that allowed to function as a medium of exchange and a store of value. Here we basically have a first banking system that was created more than 1000 years ago out of a necessity. Later, the government saw a need for control and would set up its own deposit system and issue its own certificates to have a better control over this "new" kind of money that everyone used. The Chinese government saw the benefits of this new fiat money early on as it helped to increase trade and additionally made the production of "money" easier since copper was no longer involved in the process.

A merchant would go to the government, deposit his copper and receive one of these great new certificates that he could then use just the same way as we use money today. The government on the other hand could now control the money in circulation way better and actively impact the inflation rate[11]. Later on, proper (bank) notes would be issued and the copper deposited in the "banks" would be substituted with the new bank notes. This is similar to the developments that happened in the US after the second world war. After coming out of the war the US established the so called Bretton Woods system. The system was aimed to help govern monetary relations among independent states. However, following the Vietnam war president Richard Nixon ended the international convertibility of the U.S. dollar to gold on August 15, 1971.

Another funny story about the invention of paper money that is worth telling is one including the famous explorer Marco Polo. During one of his travels through China, Polo came across paper money and subsequently learned about its production. He was fascinated about

---

[11] Though, obviously the Chinese government was far from knowledgeable on concepts as inflation rate and money supply. Concepts like quantity theory were only invented in the late 19th century. The famous Irving Fisher was one of the biggest contributors and defined a basic equation. Today it is genuinely accepted that Money supply x velocity of money = Price level x volume of transaction of goods and services.

how the Chinese can easily turn paper into money – something he has never seen before. To him this was an astonishing observation that captivated his curiosity for a while. He left China, still being fascinated about paper money and entranced as he was, he reported about his findings back home. However, once he told his stories back in Europe he was met with disbelief and ignorance rather than with interest and curiosity. It seemed impossible to the Europeans that it is achievable to create a functioning currency that is simply based on paper.

Maybe it is more obvious now to you why the Europeans failed to catch up with the Chinese innovation until many centuries later. It took Europe until the 14th century to make use of "bank notes" that were similar to the Chinese system in which precious metals were deposited to receive a note. Johannes Gutenberg introduced printing to Europe around 1439 and only in 1666 would the first paper money in Europe be issued by the Stockholm's Banco.

While I love this story and am convinced that it can tell a lot about the difference between Europe and China it is time to come back to the five dynasties. As mentioned above, China, now a multi-state system, saw many dynasties coming and going during this period. The first dynasty (Later Liang dynasty) moved its capital close to the southern borders. Moving the capital and with it the strongest military power close to the territory of the enemies is a typical thing to do and also explains the strong development of Xi'an (Chang'an) earlier in the history of China, as it was close to the enemies in the north. The name of the capital of the first of the five dynasties was Kaifeng (开封市) which is located in the province Henan, just south of the yellow river. Kaifeng will also function as capital for the later Song dynasty (960 – 1279 AD).

During most of the time the period of the five dynasties was characterized by internal conflicts, and conflicts between the southern kingdoms. While this would make great material for a movie it does not help too much in understanding present-day China and it especially won't help us in making indications about the future of China. What it helps us to understand is that China, without having a strong centre, is weak itself. This however should be nothing new to you. Therefore, we are going to fast forward through much of the history of the northern dynasties as there is nothing too interesting about this period that was not already mentioned. Instead, we focus on the things that are of greater relevance to understanding present-day China. For this, we are going to look at the Song dynasty – the successor of the five dynasties - which has more to offer than this period of transition.

# THE SONG DYNASTY (960 – 1279 AD)

The period of the Song is, similar to that of other dynasties in China's colourful history, split into two parts. The period of the northern Song and that of the southern.

It all started in the "new" capital Kaifeng. Here, the period of the northern Song dynasty begins with the absorption of the small southern states, which continued until 980 AD. The growth of the Song empire did not end here, though. Over the years the empire grew even more and at one point it even extended as far as Indonesia.

One strengthening fact at that time was the close connection between the merchants and the gentry. During the period of the Song, the revenues from taxes finally grew again which consequently helped to double the state budget in a short period of time[12]. After many years of unrest China finally started another period of economic prosperity.

---

[12] Under the Song dynasty the taxes for salt were 50% and 36% for wine! I would have not liked to live in China during this period.

During this period, the former systems of civil administration on the one hand and military administration on the other hand were abolished for a new system in which most of the administration was managed by civil officials. This change subsequently let to a demobilization of the army. More importantly though, it led to a new growth of peasant settlements in the regions of the Song which further increased the tax revenue of the state. Soldiers became merchants and former military governors joined the central administration. The Song empire became overall more efficient and made, looking back, many right choices at the beginning.

While the invention of paper money happened a while back, the Song dynasty is seen as the first legitimate government that issued paper money and deposit certificates. The government made use of this to increase inflation. They did this to meet their expenses which then again brought huge profits to the merchants who probably profited the most from these inflation measurements.

While the beginning of the Song was marked with many good developments, the end of the Song empire showed that the dynasty was still struggling. The profitable increase in tax income and revenues from the beginning vanished at the end of the northern Song dynasty (around 1065 AD) due to a change in the land ownership rules. This change ultimately caused a monopolization of land ownership under a small number of merchants which then led to a drastic decrease in tax income. By the time this became obvious to the government it was too late to reverse the land ownership and its consequences.

Many favourable developments happened during the rule of the Song dynasty. Looking at the cultural development of the northern Song dynasty we can observe that more people got educated thanks to Chinas earlier innovation of thin paper and printing. In addition to that, we see an increased support for monopolistic trade and capitalism, despite the fact that it caused a decrease in state revenue. China – one of the most famous remaining communist countries of our time – saw many of its advancements and developments during a time of open market and trade capitalism. A measure Deng Xiaoping would later reapply in order to bring China to new prosperity and dominance after many years of closed-door policy.

In addition to the cultural developments and economical advancements, the long-established idea of Confucianism (now described as Neo-Confucianism) was supporting the capitalist idea that was thriving in China.

We also see great developments and new technologies progressing during the Song period. New varieties of rice were developed in China and thanks to this surprisingly simple but revolutionary development the population of China doubled in size over the years and still kept growing thereafter.

Decreasing the military personal brought many benefits ranging from increased production to lowered cost. Despite these advances, it came with a great cost, too. Due to a decrease in military power at the end of the northern Song dynasty (we are in the later years 1125 – 1127 now) the empire saw a devastating attack on its capital from a former ally which did not only cost the capital but the entire northern part of the Song empire. The Song didn't have much to counter this attack with and suffered huge losses – even their emperor was captured during the attack. Luckily, some of the remaining forces could escape to the south and establish a new capital in Hangzhou (杭州市), formerly known as Lin'an[13].

This move to the south after the devastating defeat suffered by the northern Song marks the beginning of the southern Song.

The empire of the southern Song dynasty established itself in 1127 AD and would last for about 150 years. The new emperor was a brother of the now captive former ruler. He was also the one who decided to make Hangzhou the new capital of the southern Song.

The southern Song are now living in the south while in the north the Jurchen Jin – the invader of the northern territories – proclaimed a second kingdom as their own. We will have a look at this dynasty later in this book which will help you to better understand the

---

[13] Lin'an is now a district of Hangzhou and Hangzhou is the current capital of the Zhejiang Province (浙江省).

developments in the north. The Jurchen will conquer most of the northern territory that ranges all the way from Korea to west China. To understand the timeline, it is important to notice, that the Jurchen Jin and Liao existed parallel to the Song dynasty. Around the year 1164 both states, that of the Song and that of the Jurchen co-existed and regarded the other as one with equal rights. However, the relationship between these two states was tense from the beginning and many fights continued at the border region.

In 1233 AD the fate of the Song changed as they saw an opportunity in joining the Mongols in an attack on the Jurchen, who were still ruling in the north. During this united attack the Jurchen could be defeated but there was little time for the southern Song to relax. The Mongols did not stay an ally of the Song empire for too long and decided to attack them instead. In the years from 1273 to 1276 AD the Mongols led an attack on the now weakened southern Song empire and captured their capital at the end of this period with ease. In the end, China saw a devastating defeat and not much was left of this former empire and its glory.

The last ruler of the southern Song fled for three years and tried to get as far to the south as he could but got killed during a devastating attack on the Pearl River Delta in 1279. It was the Mongols that were now ruling over the huge Chinese territory.

# THE LIAO DYNASTY (937 – 1125 AD)

# 辽朝

The Liao dynasty lasted from 937 until 1125 AD. If you have a good eye for detail you will spot that this period is partly overlapping with that of the Song dynasty. In fact, both dynasties existed at the same time with the Liao dynasty being located in the far north which is now considered part of Mongolia, north-east China, south-east Russia, and North Korea.

If you go back to the previous section about the Song dynasty, you'll see that the northern Song ended almost at the same time as the Liao dynasty did. In fact, both were defeated by the same enemy, the Jurchen Jin.

The Jurchen first defeated the Liao dynasty. But after this first victory their army didn't stand still for too long and they continued to occupy the territory of the northern Song empire only two years after they defeated the Liao dynasty. This was a notable military achievement by the Jurchen. What was left of the Song empire after this defeat was the previously mentioned southern Song empire in the warm lands surrounding the South China Sea. In the cold north was the new empire of the Jurchen Jin. As we covered the southern Song empire in the previous section and will have a look at that of the Jurchen in the next, we will consequently look at the Liao dynasty in this chapter in separation of the other two.

In my opinion the Liao dynasty is of less importance to the history of China than the Song dynasty or that of the Jurchen Jin, as it plays a bigger role for other countries like Mongolia. Nevertheless, the Liao were an important and dominant power in the northern region that we should not just skip. The Liao empire had a mostly peaceful existence next to the Song dynasty and preferred selling horses to the Song rather than fighting them. One important development that I do want to mention at this point is that already during the time of the Liao Beijing (北京市), one of my favourite cities by far, became of first importance to the country. During this time Beijing was chosen as the capital of the Liao empire and thus managed to receive most of the wealth that was flowing into the region which helped the city to grow. This marks the foundation of the prosperous development that Beijing will undergo over the next years and we will come back to Beijing later in this book.

However, while Beijing received a lot of the money that was flowing into the region many of the tribes in the north stayed poor. One day a disastrous campaign of one of these poor tribes - that of the Jurchen – let to the attack and downfall of Beijing. The Jurchen Jin managed to capture the city and ended the Liao dynasty. Next, they decided to also end the empire of the northern Song. So, who are these Jurchen Jin, that managed to overthrow two dynasties?

# THE GREAT JIN DYNASTY (1115 – 1234 AD)

The dynasty of the Jurchen Jin is also known as that of the "Great Jin". While it can be easily mistaken for the earlier Jin dynasty when only looking at the foreign writing and sound, this dynasty differs a lot from the previously discussed dynasty.

I will use the names Jin, or great Jin, or Jurchen interchangeably as the empire of the great Jin grew out of the rebellion against the Liao which was led by the Jurchen tribe. Therefore, the empire of the Jin can be seen as that of the Jurchen.

At the time of the Jin dynasty, the different emperors that the country would see already referred to their state as Zhongguo (中國), which up until today has the same meaning: China. Or if you want to translate it more literal, Middle country, indicating that China is the centre of the world.

The great Jin would contribute a lot to the development of today's China and during their reign they oversaw many important developments that took place in the country. One is the development and revival of Confucianism which took place in both regions, that of the great Jin and that of the southern Song. The Jin changed their capital multiple times which is why we will not talk about the development of their capital like we did in previous chapters. What I do want you to notice instead, is the already tremendous size of the population which was around 50 million at its peak.

After the Liao were defeated in 1125 and the northern Song in 1127, the Jin focused more on internal development as their fear of attacks and invasion reduced over the years. With new territory under the rule of the Jin, they faced a new enemy though. The Mongols. Due to the new threat of a Mongol invasion the Jin would contribute to the development of the Great Wall of China and make it a primary defence system against their northern threat. It is during this time that the Great Wall was used to keep the Mongols - and their founder and first leader Genghis Kahn - out. Many stories of the wars with the Mongol leader Genghis Kahn would date back to the time of the great Jin.

You already know the end of the story but let's have a look at it again from the perspective of the great Jin to understand this dynasty a bit better. During the 13ᵗʰ century, the Jin dynasty saw more and more attacks in their north from the Mongols. With the additional help of the southern Song, the Jin faced a war on two fronts at the same time and got defeated in the end when Öged ei Kahn, the successor of Genghis Kahn, invaded the country together with southern Song in 1232 AD. The last emperor of the great Jin committed suicide in 1234, when he saw himself defeated. The southern Song and the Mongols started their war soon after this, after a dispute over the Jin territory escalated. With the southern Song being eventually defeated the Mongols now ruled over all of China. This period is considered as that of the Yuan dynasty.

# THE YUAN DYNASTY (1271 – 1368 AD)

The Yuan dynasty is different than the various dynasties that existed before because now a Mongol leader, Kublai Khan, is ruling over most of what is now present-day China. This means, that China is now ruled by a non-Han leader and a non-Chinese for the first time in history. In fact, at this point in time we could speak of a Mongol epoch, rather than a Chinese. However, this period is equally important for the development of China as the many dynasties before and therefore important to talk about.

China, which was now ruled by the Mongols, was treated as an independent empire under the Mongolian rule rather than seen as a part of the Mongol empire itself. Quite remarkable is the fact that the Mongol empire, which was founded by the famous and well-known Genghis Kahn, is for now the largest contiguous empire in the world.

It is hard to perfectly fit a timeline onto this dynasty, as it grew over time into the empire it was in the end, but it is generally accepted that the Yuan dynasty started in 1271 after Kublai Khan gave China the name "Great Yuan".

Beijing (北京市) was chosen to be the new capital of this Chinese-Mongol-empire and the Mongol leaders named it Dadu which stands for "Great Capital" – An appropriate name for a city like Beijing. Naming Beijing the new capital was beneficial for the Mongols as it was geographically close to Mongolia. However, Beijing had to be reconstructed as much of the old city was destroyed during the previous attacks on this pearl in the east. Therefore, it is not now, but instead during the rule of the Ming and Qing dynasties that Beijing will find its later glory. Nevertheless, it already plays an important role at this point in history. Since the Ming and Qing dynasties will have a bigger impact on Beijing, we will have a more in-depth look at the development of Beijing later in this book to better match the development of the city with the dynasty in charge of it.

If we focus on the Yuan dynasty again, we see, that under the rule of Kublai Khan, the population was now divided into four different groups. The first group is that of the Mongols themselves. The class of the Mongol was of course seen as the ruling class and therefore also enjoyed the most privileges. From now on they were the ones who controlled the military and who got elected into official government positions across the country. The second is the group of people from central Asia like the Uighurs and Turkish people. The third and the fourth group is that of the northern and southern Chinese, respectively. While the last two make two different groups their social status was more or less equal.

It is interesting to see that at this time the northern and southern Chinese were the classes with the lowest social status and even intermarriage with these classes was prohibited for the Mongols. The Uighurs from central Asia enjoyed work as merchants or translators for the ruling Mongols which made them important and indispensable to their rulers. This is quite different to the way things are today. If we compare it with today, Uighurs are considered as one of the ethnic groups that suffers the most in China, with an already bad economic situation in west China and their Islamic believe being a thorn in the eye of the Communist government. Han-Chinese on the other hand are seen as the highest class in today's China as most people believe that Han-Chinese are the "real" Chinese.

During the period of the Yuan, China (or rather the Mongol empire) engaged in multiple wars over its existence. All of them happened far away from home and came with little actual impact on the daily life of many Chinese in the beginning. Kublai Khan led a fight against the Japanese in 1281, Myanmar in 1282, Cambodia in 1284, and even reached as far as Indonesia in 1292. A true conqueror.

The earlier invention of Gunpowder helped the Mongols in defeating their foreign enemies the same way it helped them earlier in defeating the southern Song dynasty.

In the end, despite the fact that many Chinese did not participate in the war in the beginning, they still had to suffer severe consequences from the aftereffects of the wars. Due to the many wars and the decrease in trade during the Yang dynasty (Mongol-) China was faced with a wave of impoverishment of its population.

The Chinese already suffered due to their low social status but an additional change in the monetary system would make the situation even worse for them. Due to the high war expenses, China saw a lot of its metal currency flowing out of the country which subsequently lead to an increase in government printed paper money to make up for this outflow. This made paper money the now predominant medium of exchange in all of the Mongol-Chinese empire.

However, the government was not too experienced regarding monetary policy, and still had a lot to learn about the consequences of different policies. As the value of the paper money depreciated the government did not know how to react. Nothing seemed to stop this depreciation which led to an even more dramatic impoverishment of the people all across the country. This might have been the first hyperinflation in history.

We heard the stories about Marco Polo earlier in this book. Most of these stories talk about the great developments in China rather than the increasing poverty because travellers such as Polo would be taken care of and they would thus see little of this hardship. Instead, they were blinded by the spectacular temples and were treated superior to the normal population which made them fail to see the impoverishment that actually existed in China at that time.

The increased poverty also left its mark on the people and the country at this point in time. The people were suffering and they blamed the government for this. Similar to the many dynasties before the increasing hardship of the people led to growing turmoil and unrest in the country. It is assumed that in 1329 around 7.5 million out of the more than 50 million people living in China were starving[14].

And while it is just words here, at this point in time the situation was very real, drastic, and extreme! The escalation of the uprising came surprising to the Mongols who struggled to cope with it early on. The Mongols were conquerors, not governors and thus did not know how to react after the country was hit by hyperinflation. This time, the new gentry was on the supporting side of the Mongols rather than that of the poor as most of the attacks were directed towards the rich in particular, not only the Mongols. Thus, supporting the Mongols against the uprisings meant fighting for their own lives. Despite its

---

[14] These numbers might not be completely accurate but represent a good approximation of the population and the number of people starving in relationship to it.

intensity the uprising could be stopped for a while and the Mongols found a short period of rest.

In the end, after a few years of rest the fights started again. As the situation in China did not improve, it seems not too surprising that new fights erupted which led to the ultimate end of the Yuan dynasty and the Mongol rule over China.

The last ten years of the Yuan empire were full of small battles and in 1368 Beijing was captured by the uprising peasants. The Mongol rulers had no other chance but to flee to Mongolia to find a safe haven back home. In the end the Mongol dynasty was defeated by the peasants of the country who took back what belonged to them.

# THE MING DYNASTY (1368 – 1644 AD)

# 明朝

O nce again the peasants revolted and the Mongols were now pushed back to where they came from – the steppes in the far north. At this point, China was finally ruled again by a Chinese person. Over the years the once gone feeling of nationalism came back and with it many changes to the country. The new empire was called Ming and would last for the next 300 years and leave many marks on the country.

During the rule of the Ming, the Mongols never tried to attack and reoccupy China again. Instead, they decided to stay in Mongolia from now on. The troubles for the Chinese did not end, though. New problems emerged with Japanese pirates attacking the south and the east of China in the form of organized raids. Cities were plundered and destroyed. This wouldn't be the last time that Japan would attack China and by far not the worst. It was bad enough however to leave its mark on the country. The above-mentioned Japanese pirates are one of the main reasons why many cities moved inwards, and a big and strong Chinese navy was never created. Nothing could stop these pirates for now and thus escaping into the mainland seemed to be the best option available for the Chinese families living at the coastal area. It would take until 1467 AD – a time of turmoil in Japan – that the raids from the Japanese pirates stopped. None of the credits for this can go to China, though.

During later years of the Ming dynasty more European settlers would come to China with their boats, creating similar destruction to the Japanese pirates. This led many of the Chinese to believe that the Europeans, too, were barbarians and pirates and not better than the Japanese. Actually, they were not too wrong with this assumption. In fact, up until this time the Arabic and Chinese emerged as the most civilized empires in the world with many of the other countries being decades behind.

During the rule of the Ming empire the population of the country grew fast and new advancements in rice farming helped to almost double the production of rice in just a few years. I think it is important to note at this point that these improvements in particular in agriculture and farming helped to increase the population size tremendously[15]. Additionally, the advancements in rice farming helped to decrease the number of malaria mosquitoes in the south. Farmers started to put fishes into the wet rice fields to help with fertilization and to have additional food production for themselves. They did not initially plan it but these fishes incidentally helped to make most of south China malaria free and more and more inhabitable since the fish removed most of the mosquitos and thus one of the main problems in the south. In fact, this agricultural revolution of the Ming will lead to a population revolution in 1550 AD. The increase in population let to

---

[15] Actually, agricultural development is still one of the most important factors for emerging markets today.

a consequential increase in urbanization and cities grew now to never before seen dimensions.

We further see an increase in book printing during the time of the Ming dynasty which for the first time made it extremely easy to get access to books and gradually the "art" of reading spread from the scholars to businessmen and finally even farmers. Over the years more and more people became literate.

While I cannot proclaim myself to be a big enthusiast of porcelain, I do find it important to mention at this point that the famous blue and white porcelain became famous during the period of the Ming. Porcelain itself was for a long time a mysterious material for many. It combined a translucent glare with an extreme hardness that allowed Chinese artisans to make extremely thin ceramics. The European elite couldn't get enough of it, which came to the benefit of the (now famous) pottery town of Jingdezhen (景德镇市), in central China.

This extremely fine porcelain was sought-after from all over the world. King August II of Poland and Duke of Lithuania[16] was probably one of the biggest admirers of the Chinese-made porcelain with its glass-like surface. Apparently, during the first year of his rule he paid out more than 100,000 thalers - enough to pay the annual salaries of a thousand skilled craftsmen.

Despite his admiration for porcelain, production wasn't easy and it seemed for a long time that no one could replicate the famous Chinese porcelain. It would take until 1708 until the Europeans would be able to produce porcelain of similar quality themselves – It was Meissen Porcelain which became known as the first European porcelain of similar quality, able to compete with its Chinese counterpart.

Not only art, porcelain, and literature developed during the rule of the Ming but also the development of Beijing continued. Thus, I want to keep my earlier promise and talk a bit more about Beijing at this point.

---

[16] Also known as Augustus the Strong of Saxony.

In a family dispute that is worth a book by itself, the king of Beijing and son of the emperor of China, found himself fighting for the throne when his father and the actual heir to the throne both died. While the first son of the heir was named as the new emperor his time on the throne was limited. As a consequence of the two earlier deaths, the king of Beijing saw his chance and marched to Nanjing with his army, captured the city, and burned down its many palaces. He then massacred the young king and most of his supporters. By the time he returned to Beijing, the new capital now, he was already the new emperor of the Ming empire.

With Beijing as the new capital many new striking palaces were built to reflect the glory of the new emperor and the city. The most famous being the forbidden city in the heart of Beijing. The forbidden city was constructed during early years while Beijing was still being rebuilt which allowed for the construction of the building that we know up until today for its mammoth proportions. Thousands of workers had to suffer for years to build the forbidden city the way Kuai Xiang (蒯祥) planned it to be, which would later function as residence for the emperor[17]. The forbidden city is an enormous temple complex with 980 buildings and a size of more than 72 hectares or almost 135 football fields.

Another important development that took place during the period of the Ming dynasty was the southward expansion and the explorations made by Zheng He (郑和), probably the most famous explorer that China ever had. Zheng He was not only a Muslim but also a eunuch and explored the southern sea and the many common trading routes of the Chinese empire. He went to Southeast Asian regions like Java and travelled as far as west Asia and even east Africa and Arabia during his explorations. While the explorations of Zheng He were only of short duration and ended around 1415 AD they taught us again about the enormous developments that China made and China's superior know-how at the time. It is reported that the ships Zheng He used for

---

[17] The construction lasted from 1406 until 1420.

his voyages were about 127 meters long and 52 wide[18]! This makes them the largest wooden ships in history. Nothing the European conquerors could ever match in size.

China, which by now is one of the most important countries in the world, was by all means a prosperous trade centre. Porcelain was manufactured and sent all over the world and China became more involved with global trade. This trade brought in massive amounts of silver and gold and flooded the country with prosperity.

Another important but less glamourous development was the confiscation of land estates from private people by the government in the attempt to centralise the control more and to grow the power of the emperor and his government. These new state-owned buildings were then rented out and thus generated a new income stream for the government.

In addition to finding alternative income sources, the government also developed on the human rights front. It is worth mentioning that slavery was abolished during the Ming dynasty. Funny enough, this change of action caused a subsequent increase in the number of peasants and provided the country with new tax-paying workers.

However good the situation for the people, the regime of the Ming was characterized by internal conflicts about the rule of the empire and additional internal struggles between rival cliques.

With the conflicts over the power came the introduction of a secret police that was set up by the eunuchs and cliques in Beijing in order to influence the decision making in a, let's call it "alternative way". This secret police functioned more and more like a dictatorial organ and caused many people to either disappear completely or to be arrested. The control of the eunuchs and cliques reach so far that by 1505 AD the new fifteen-year-old heir to the throne was under complete control by them. By 1521 AD the ineffective reign of the young emperor ended after his early death and he was replaced by another fifteen-year-old emperor who was as much a marionette of the eunuchs and cliques as

---

[18] That is 442 feet in length and a width of about 170 feet.

the previous one. After him followed a ten-year-old emperor, who was equally influenced and controlled by the same marionette-players.

At the same time the relationship with Japan grew colder after Japan tried to occupy Korea and had to be sent back by the Chinese. In return, the Japanese plundered and destroyed more of the coastal towns of eastern China, leaving behind many areas of destruction.

On top of this came an increase in the disputes between the cliques who were still trying to beat each other at their power game in the capital.

Over the years things were heating up for the Ming dynasty with internal conflicts increasing and the economic situation declining as a consequence. Additionally, the newly started war with Japan left its mark on the country, which caused increasing financial problems. Adding to this was a further damage on the economy due to natural calamities in the region which caused agricultural production to drop dramatically.

Like always bad news comes never alone. Looking at this it is not too surprising that the final years of the dynasty were plagued with wide-spread draughts and famine. And like many times before in the history of China, the increase in poverty and breakdown of a functioning government lead to disputes and turmoil in the country. At the peak of the uproar, the ethnic group of the Manchus, which originated from the Jurchen, lead attacks against the government in Beijing. Up until now the Manchus are an ethnic minority in China but due to the bad economic situation, they gained a lot of support from other sides. In a final uprising the government was brought down in 1644 and a new, Manchu-led government was established to lead the country from now on.

# THE QING DYNASTY (1644 – 1911 AD)

# 清朝

With the Ming dynasty at an end, the last dynasty that was led by a Han-Chinese person was over. The new empire, that of the Qing, was established by the ethnic group of the Manchu and would last up until the year 1911. As we are reaching further into the present, we will look more closely at the developments that happened in China as they become more and more relevant for the second part of this book – present day China.

The Manchus took advantage of the situation that emerged at the end of the Ming dynasty and managed to gain control over China despite their small number. Already one year after they gained control over the country, the new rulers in Beijing decided that all of China should follow the old customs of the Manchus and introduced a new law that demanded the Chinese to wear a special kind of pigtail hairstyle and typical Manchurian clothing. It just seems a lot like the new government tried hard to offend the national pride of the many Han-Chinese in the country. If that was their intention, they were very successful at it for sure.

Not uncommon and already of importance during other dynasties is the introduction of a law that forbid the intermarriage between Manchus and Han-Chinese to keep the now dominating Manchu race "pure". The Manchus also set up a so called "eight banners" system in the attempt to segregate themselves from the "impure" Chinese. The "eight banners" were military institutions that only allowed membership after a careful selection based on traditional Manchu skills. This naturally favoured the people with Manchu roots. Members of these banners were given special privileges which helped the Manchus to stay in power and control critical functions.

The Qing also managed to grow the already geographically big China in land-size as they conquered areas to the west and north, which helped them to spread their influence further. The areas in the west being Xinjiang and Tibet. Mongolia being the area of the northern expansion. Later in this book we will have a quick look at the developments between Tibet and China. The current claim that Tibet belongs to China originates from this period amongst other things.

During the eighteenth century the power of the Qing started to decline and this decline would continue to reach all the way into the twentieth century. While the Qing dynasty improved itself until the middle of the eighteenth century, it started to decline around the same time the French revolution took place in Europe. Not indicating that there was any correlation between these two events. The Qing dynasty was rather struggling with a never-ending increase in its population which grew over the years almost exponentially to an enormous size. While the Qing counted around 100 million people during its beginning this numbers grew over time. At the beginning of the eighteenth century around 275 million people lived under the rule of the Qing. By 1850 the number already crossed the 400 million mark and the growth did not stop. Right now, more than 1.4 billion people live in China[19]. During the Qing dynasty most of these people still worked as farmers spread across the country. They lived outside of the cities, were not involved in the political wheeling and dealing and lived a through and through simple life. Despite this fact, the agricultural production could not keep up with the increase in population.

Additionally, China also faced more and more foreigners coming to Macao and Guangzhou in order to trade with this massive east Asian

---

[19] These numbers might be subject to rounding. Nevertheless, they help you to get a general understanding of the population size during the time of the Qing dynasty.

nation state. Generally, foreigners were not allowed to enter the country, though. The foreign merchants were only allowed to trade with the so called "Hong" in the above-mentioned cities, a specific group that was holding a monopolistic position to trade with the foreigners. The Hong then paid taxes to the state. A business that made both, the state and the Hong rich by every measure.

We can't really talk about the Qing dynasty without talking about the two opium wars that took place during this period and I think now is a good time to do so. In the nineteenth century, around 1839 the first opium war started.

Going back in time we can see that over the years, China saw an increase in trade with foreign countries, as its fine silks and flavourful teas were sought after all over the world. Porcelain could already be produced in Europe and while still exported, the focus shifted to other products. While the British and the Dutch were very interested in buying tea and silk from the Chinese, the Chinese were not that interested in foreign products. They instead showed more interest in owing silver and gold. During the beginning of the eighteenth-century opium began to be important to China - one of the few foreign products the Chinese showed interest in. Soon after the British figured this out, they saw the opportunity to enrich themselves. Their trading company, the so-called East India Company, started to smuggle opium into China. One reason for introducing opium to China was to counter the increasing silver inflow into the country.

While opium offered merchants a new opportunity to make money, farmers were the ones that had to suffer. The opium trade had negative consequences for most of the farmers because they could not keep up with the following increase in taxes. Additionally, illegal opium, together with the legally available opium spread across China and deteriorated its trade surplus on the one hand and turned China's citizens into addicts on the other hand. A disastrous development for the Chinese. The British were happy that their efforts payed off; they finally found a product that they could sell to the Chinese. Understandably, they Chinese were not that happy. Thus, attempts were made from the Chinese side to talk to the British and to Queen Victoria to stop the illegal opium flow into the country. To no one's surprise nothing happened. The British enjoyed this profitable trade too much and showed no interest in negotiating with the Chinese or to stop their highly profitable operation.

As a consequence, and as a last resort the Chinese government confiscated all opium that enter through Guangzhou – the gateway to China. Only at this time did the British respond. However, their response was different than what the Chinese wished for. The British send their established, strong, and experienced navy to the South Chinese Sea to solve the conflict the old-fashioned way. The powerful navy fleet of the British bombed the coastal cities in the south and made clear that they are the stronger party at the table. The Qing, who only had a weak navy and no experience in sea fight, could only watch their cities burn. In 1842, after multiple defeats, the British ceded Hong Kong Island. They then forced the Chinese to sign a treaty, the so called "Treaty of Nanjing"[20], which granted them the control over the important port region in perpetuity. The treaty also included the control over five other important ports in China. As an end result Guangzhou, Xiamen, Ningbo, and Shanghai all started being under British control from now on. While the British left behind their beautiful Victorian architecture China was the clear loser in this unequal treaty that numbed the country.

I guess that China was still lucky, though. China did not become a colony and could at least withstand the colonial powers long enough. Things could have turned out way worse and China could have ended the same way Myanmar or India did after British rule.

Understandably, over the years the relationship between China and Britain grew extremely cold and the inflow of illegal opium did continue as this was a highly profitable operation for the British empire. And that was the only thing that mattered to the British. Around 1856 AD the Chinese pulled the trigger again to protect its citizen and stopped ships on the suspicion of smuggling. The British with their

---

[20] Also referred to as "Treaty of Nanking", Nanking being the old name for Nanjing.

slightly bad temper were outrageous about the developments in the Pearl River Delta and send a new army to show the Chinese their limitations. The Qing, who stilled missed out on having a sizable navy, were unable to defend themselves at this point, too.

The new challenges coming from outside China were coming unexpected and fast and the Qing dynasty was not prepared for them. I guess you could say that at this point in time China reached an all-time low in its History. This time the British decided to enter China as a consequence of their action and to march to Beijing. They landed in Tianjin and their military power and dominance allowed them to "negotiate" another unfair treaty with China. This time, the "Treaty of Tianjin" (previously known as "Treaty of Tientsin") gave the British control over Kowloon, the land surrounding Hong Kong Island, legislative power in Beijing, freedom to navigate along the Yangtze river (扬子江 also known as 长江 in Chinese) and it finally legalised the British opium imports. In addition to that, eleven more Chinese ports would be opened for foreign trade and be effectively under British rule. Probably the only reason why the British did not conquer all of China at this point was because they were too busy with India on the one hand and enjoyed the huge profit they made with the opium business on the other hand. This period of new fights about opium flooding China is today known as the second opium war.

With China just being one step away of becoming a British colony at this point and being completely under British control, the trade balances that China accumulated over the decades deteriorated. At this point in time the Qing dynasty could do nothing but watch how European goods entered the country. China was not able to set essential import taxes on them or profit from those trades in any other way. A new financial crisis was hitting China which now saw an increasing impoverishment of its people. Old patterns repeated themselves and at this time China saw the number of revolts – mainly led by the peasants – increasing over the years. At all fronts there were old problems rising and new problems erupting and the country was once again in a state of uncertainty and turmoil. This time though, most of the risings in the country didn't follow a clear political aim as there was not much the government could do as most of the problems were caused by the British – and they were unlikely to leave anytime soon.

Adding to all these problems was a growing conflict with Japan which would last until 1945. Japan, which not only became more westernized over the years but also self-confident, started a period of imperialism that would shape most of the Asia we know today. By the year 1876 the Japanese started to penetrate into Korea, which was still under Chinese protection. Ten years later, by 1885 Japan proclaimed that Korea would now be a joint area between them and China. Another ten years ahead in time, now we write the year 1894, the first Sino-Japanese war started[21]. At the centre of this war was the control over Korea. The war was going on for more than half a year but the armies of the Chinese had no success in defeating the Japanese. By 1895 the Qing government saw no other option but to sign a peace treaty with the Japanese. Again, the Qing military had no means to defend the country, almost making this numbness a characteristic of the late Qing dynasty.

The Qing dynasty did not only lose the Korean territory but also control over the north-east Chinese region that was known as Manchuria. In addition to that, Taiwan, which was conquered and annexed during the early days of the Qing dynasty in 1683 was now given to the Japanese empire along with Penghu and the Liaodong Peninsula.

The period of the late Qing dynasty marks a devastating time in Chinese history and missing the opportunities to modernize the military and country only made things worse. Gradually people realized that things needed to change in order for China to maintain its importance in the world. Japan, which was previously only seen as a barbarian state filled with pirates, easily managed to defeat the Chinese with its western technology.

---

[21] As you can probably guess, numbering this war to be the first indicates that there will be a second war. We will talk about the second Sino-Japanese war later in this book.

By 1908 AD, after multiple rebellions (The boxer rebellion being the most famous one), both the empress and the emperor died in 1908, leaving behind an unstable government that was now ruled by a two-year-old boy. Leaving a country that was under increasing threat from outside in the hands of a two-year-old boy, in addition to the failures at home, brought further instability to the country. If it wouldn't be for the rivalry between the colonial powers China might have been annexed already.

New uprisings started all over China. With the first uprisings starting, the first cities declared their independence. First in Hunan and then soon after Wuchang. Wuchang proclaimed a separate central government by October 10, 1911. They called themselves the Republic of China and Sun Yat-sen (孙逸仙), the leader of the revolutionaries was declared President. After the ruling powers in Beijing understood that the imperial house and the monarchy could no longer be defended an edict was issued in which the government declared that the country would from now on be a constitutional state. This was February 12th 1912 – a day that would change China forever.

The more than 2000-year-old imperial China came to a bitter end. China had lost its former glory and was being ripped apart first by the British and then by the Japanese. The Qing dynasty was over and many years of familiar instability and turmoil returned to the country.

# THE REPUBLIC OF CHINA (1912 – 1949 AD)

# 中华民国

Following the Qing dynasty we have the Republic of China. The republic would last until the year 1949 and would see the two World Wars taking place. The period of the Republic of China would also be characterized with many changes that take place in the country and all around the world. In addition to that, the capitalist influence of western countries would grow within China. Just as an example, Land would now be considered capital and used as an investment vehicle just as it is the case nowadays in many places all over the world.

One of the biggest changes that the country faced was that it was without an emperor. The cliques - who previously always tried to grow in importance by influencing the emperor - saw themselves without a clear objective now as they had no one to influence. The "new" persons of superior influence were the military officials and the governors. These two groups saw their personal wealth grow since many turned to them with bribes, trying to corrupt them and influence their decision making. Most of the time with success. Corruption was at an all-time high after the dissolution of the empire and would remain a problem in China up until today.

While an elite group of officials and merchants still existed, many of them would only be considered middle class. In addition to that, a small proletariat would exist in the country. However, the majority of people would be uneducated peasants who lived outside of the cities.

In order to escape these poor conditions, the former revolutionary leader and father of the republic Sun Yat-sen laid down a strategy that consisted of three stages to achieve new progress and prosperity. This famous work was called "the three principles of the people" or 三民主义 as it is known in China. The three principles are nationalism or

Mínzú (民族主義) democracy or Mínquán (民權主義) and government of the people, also called Mínshēng (民生主義). Sun Yat-sen was convinced that China would reach new prosperity and become again a great nation if it followed these three principles.

In his writings Sun further describes how China will need to pass through three phases before it will finally succeed as a country again. The phase of the struggle in which China will need to fight in order to overcome the old system, the phase of the educative rule which was similar to an authoritarian system with democratic influence, and the final phase in which China will become a democratic nation, the phase of a truly democratic government.

While Confucianism and Taoism still spread across the country they were by no mean as dominant as they used to be in the past. Instead, pragmatism was finding its ground in the country. Another philosophical doctrine that found ground in China and that spread rapidly was Marxism.

The early years of the republic were not only marked with demonstrations but also with risings from military units and single attempts throughout the country to gain independence from the government. One incident took place as early as 1912 in which Guangzhou declared itself independent from the Republic of China. In addition to that, we can observe multiple desperate attempts of the "old classes" to reintroduce an imperial house, which up until now helped them to maintain their power.

Yuan Shikai (袁世凱), a military and government official, who played an important role in overthrowing the Qing dynasty entered the stage. With the aim to unite the country, Sun Yat-sen decided to step down from his position as President of the republic to make space for Yuan Shikai to unite and lead the country. Yuan previously helped to overthrow the emperor with his troops and now, after being elected President, he ruled the country with his military power, ignoring most of the republican institution that Sun Yat-sen previously established. With the rule of Yuan, though, China was now officially recognized as a new state by foreign countries which gave his rule additional legitamcy.

Following the establishment of the Republic of China, Britain demanded that Tibet and China would be separated. While China and Tibet would been separated for a while, Tibet returned to China soon after the second World War.

While we are on the topic of China's border politics we can have a look at China's and Russia's interest over Mongolia. In 1911 Russian interest dominated in the outer Mongolia region which led to the so-called Russo-Chinese treaty which was signed in 1913, in which outer Mongolia was recognized as an independent state and Inner Mongolia would remain a part of the Chinese realm. With the outbreak of the first world war the Japanese attacked Qingdao, the German centre in China and sieged it in 1914, increasing Japanese influence in the region. These early disputes between China and Japan started an early opposition from Students in Beijing.

If this wouldn't be enough trouble already, Yuan took advantage of his new position as President. With Sun Yat-sen finally out of the picture, Yuan seized the opportunity to solidify his position of power. Yuan Shikai saw intensifying attempts of the parliament in Beijing to establish a permanent institution and to gain control over him. For Yuan this could mean losing the power over the country in a new open election. He thus made all possible attempts to turn the country back into an empire. In 1914 he already succeeded by putting all decision-making power into his own hands and by naming himself president for life. In 1915 he then persuaded what was left of the parliament and named himself the emperor of China. As a consequence of this many of the states declared themselves independent and quickly returned back to Warlord rule.

While Sun was still fighting for a democratic country, the colonial powers were happy about the developments and the turmoil in China as they would profit more from a divided country. They thus opposed Yuan as emperor to intensify the conflict. As a response to this intense opposition Yuan decided to reversed his course of action and decided to become president of the republic again rather than emperor. Soon after this decision he died a natural cause.

While China was still a Republic it was too late to turn back in time. By now already five provinces declared themselves independent and China was faced with a new period of Warlords. By the year 1917 Sun Yat-sen successfully instituted a revolutionary base in Guangzhou, aiming to reunite the nation. Just two years later he succeeded and re-established the national party in Beijing.

On May 4th 1919 the intellectual modernization of China began. University students gathered in Beijing to demonstrate against the government – this movement is today known as the May Fourth Movement (五四运动). The students demonstrated against the imperialist culture that existed and the governments reaction to the consequences of the Treaty of Versailles.

The Treaty of Versailles, probably one of the most famous peace treaties, brought the first world war to an end. It was officially signed on June 28th 1919, due to the importance of the day being the exact day archduke Franz Ferdinand was assassinated five years earlier. This treaty however was not signed by the Chinese because Japan did not return the previously "liberated" territory to them. The catch was that after the Germans arrived in Versailles at the end of April it became clear that the previously German territory[22] in China would be officially handed over to the Japanese.

The May 4th demonstration escalated after the police started to attack the students and jailed some of them. The strikes heightened when first the students and then the general public boycotted Japanese imports as a consequence. By now Japan was hated throughout all of China. It should be noted here that while the May 4th Movement happened in 1919, its fellowship grew since the first World war starting around the year 1915. The movement lasted for almost two more years, ending around 1921.

---

22 The German forces occupied Qingdao from 1898 to 1914. During their occupation the Germans established a brewery, the Germania Brewery, in 1903 which would later become the now famous Tsingtao Brewery.

One of the consequences of the May Fourth Movement was an almost complete collapse of the leading powers in Beijing. All of these developments finally led to the founding of the Communist Party of China (CPC) in 1921. The Communist Party was founded by Chen Duxiu (陳獨秀) and Li Dazhao (李大釗) and rapidly grew in the number of its followers thanks to promises like lowering taxation and giving land to the peasants. With the help of the Soviet Union, Sun cooperated with the Communist Party to reunite the north and south of China. The Russians also helped in establishing a working administration in this country similar to that of the Soviet Union. However, Sun Yat-sen died unexpectedly in 1925 leaving behind an unfinished task.

Sun's successor, was Chiang Kai-shek (蔣介石). Soon after taking the leadership he celebrated early success in defeating the remaining independent leaders in the north and in reuniting China. But the success of Chiang was not long lasting and a fatal mistake would change things very soon. Out of the fear that the communist will take over he decided to attack them first, which led to thousands losing their lives. The Russian advisers were dismissed. Chiang established his government in Nanjing (previously Nanking) in 1927 and from now on followed a new objective of defeating the communist once and for all[23].

By 1928 Chiang managed to completely reunite the last parts of China. However, the fight between the communist on the one hand and the Chiang-led government on the other hand continued and would continue until 1949.

The conflict would be spread into two stages. The first lasting from 1927 and 1937 and the second from 1946 to 1950. In-between, we have the second Sino-Japanese War which took place from 1937 until 1945. We will come back to these two civil wars later in this section as

---

[23] History would later prove Chiang right, as the communist would indeed take over later during the 20th century. However, it seems like a self-fulfilling prophecy as it were his attacks that moved the needle.

it will play an important role for the establishment of the People's Republic of China.

The Nanjing-based nationalist government would have many small successes such as bringing the import and export duties back under Chinese control which generated a new income stream for the government. The new found government would however continue to have growing disputes with Japan, which still enjoyed the benefits of occupying important Chinese territory. The Japanese did not stop occupying coastal areas in China and also started to smuggle goods further into the rural parts of the country, spreading propaganda and manipulating the Chinese currency.

By 1937 these conflicts escalated into a full-scale war. In 1937 Japan not only occupied the formerly German Qingdao but also started to occupy Beijing and the regions between these two. Shanghai was the next city on the list to be occupied. On their way the Japanese captured Nanjing, which caused the government to resettle. By now, the Japanese had captured most of the coastal regions in China, cutting off the country from important imports and wealth-creating exports. Not stopping there, the Japanese went further, now westwards, capturing also what was inside the country.

The Chinese on the other hand had no means to defend themselves and could only watch how Japan was taking over more and more areas of the country. Those who had the chance fled to the west. With most of the east of China now being under Japanese rule, the old governments were changed into new puppet governments that followed Japanese order.

By now Japan's power in the east has grown to a point at which the country felt strong and confident enough to take on the western powers and their colonies in Asia. Japan attacked almost everywhere, sending soldiers to Hong Kong, Singapore, Indo-China and leading attacks on places like Pearl Harbour. By now it seemed that nothing could stop East Asia from becoming Japanese.

By 1945 the second World War was ending in Europe, but Japan was far from stopping their quest to conquer all of Asia. But the World was about to change forever on the 6th and 9th of August 1945. The United States sent two nuclear bombs. The first one on Hiroshima, the second one on Nagasaki. With the two nuclear bombs came the collapse of Japan.

Immediately after the attacks on Japan, China was unexpectedly free again. No colonial powers, no foreign invaders, no Japan. Japan, now defeated, posed no threat to China anymore and the country was finally able to be itself again.

However, at this point, we should go back in time for a second to have a more in-depth look at the earlier development of communism in the country. These developments will become of relevance when we want to understand the fall of the Republic of China in 1949 and the two civil wars. The influence of communism in China grew after its early successes in the Soviet Union. Chinese intellectuals saw it as given, that the concepts of communism could easily be applied to a country like China.

The communist party itself was created out of a movement at my alma mater, Peking University, where the up until then unknown Mao Zedong (毛泽东) worked. If you remember, this political movement grew fast over the years and even collaborated with Sun Yat-sen and later Chiang Kai-shek and his party until 1927. This was the same year that Mao Zedong, who was back in his home in Hunan, wrote down some of his own ideas of how communism can be successful. He was convinced that in order for it to be successful it had to be based upon the peasants and farmers.

If you remember what we learned earlier, Chiang was getting worried when he saw the communist movement growing and separated himself from the earlier collaboration in 1927 and attack the communist out of fear that their power would grow too big. In 1934, as a consequence of the attacks, the remaining communist started what is now known as the "Long March" where the communist fought their way through northwest China. One of the participants was Deng Xiaoping (邓小平), the future paramount leader of China and one of the greatest politicians of all time.

Only the attack of Japan brought the nationalist and communist back together on one table. However, this was only for a short and limited amount of time. At the end of the war the nationalist returned to power, but the communist won the hearts of the people outside of the cities. Out of the wish to change the political direction of the country a civil war started again and by the end of 1948 almost all of mainland China was under the control of the communist.

The nationalist on the other hand retreated to Taiwan to escape the communist soldiers and their deadly revenge. By the end of the civil war almost two million fleeing nationalist lived on this little Island in the south. The new government of Taiwan almost perfectly resembled the Chinese government before the civil war. We should note at this point that Chiang himself saw Taiwan as a province of China rather than an independent state which is why he ironically called his government the "Central Government of China". Over the years the "Taiwanese" government manage to create a stable currency and with eliminating most of the corruption it brought new prosperity to this small island.

Most of the early Taiwanese see themselves as Chinese as they almost all originated from mainland China and only the Americans (and also the Japanese) favoured the idea that Taiwan should become an independent and democratic state. Taiwan however, cannot neglect its historical roots. This is even genuinely accepted by the US. The United States, under the so called Taiwan relations act, admit that Taiwan geographically belongs to China. They do however state that they want a reunification to happen peacefully. If Mainland China decides to attack the law would require them to come to Taipei's assistance. Beijing, however, sees Taiwan as a reminder for the humiliations it suffered at the hands of foreign powers.

The failure to exploit existing ways to develop the country before the first World War and the constant occupation from foreign colonial powers occupied almost all of the energy of the nationalist from its establishment until its fall. While Chiang and his nationalist movement escaped to Taiwan, mainland China grew under its communist rule.

The success of mainland China rather came from the fact that China was now free from foreign invaders than its form of government, though. Sometimes a stable government is the most important in order to succeed as a country. And while China became a communist and thus marxist country, typical Chinese traits are still omnipresent in the minds and hearts of the people. China is thus not a second Soviet Union but had and still has to follow its own path.

# THE PEOPLE'S REPUBLIC OF CHINA
## (1949 - PRESENT)

# 中华人民共和国

I am writing about the period of the "People's Republic of China" with some excitement. This is not because it is the most recent period in China's long history, but it is the period in which one of my personal heroes, Deng Xiaoping (邓小平), led China to its current success. A development that might have not happened without him. It is the period is which China will finally start to recover from Europe's negative influence and humiliation, but also a period in which many of China's old traditions are overshadowed by the new ruling communism.

The People's Republic of China begins with the victory of the communist over the nationalist and with the nationalist's subsequent escape to Taiwan.

On October 1st 1949 Mao Zedong proclaimed the People's Republic of China from the top of Tiananmen square. While standing on top of Tiananmen Gate Mao Zedong declared: "The Chinese have always been a great, courageous and industrious nation; it is only in modern times that they have fallen behind. And that was due entirely to oppression and exploitation by foreign imperialism and domestic reactionary governments ... Ours will no longer be a nation subject to insult and humiliation. We have stood up."

Soon after this the communist demonstrated their strength for the first time in the Korean War.

The war originally started as a by-product of the Cold War that was going on between the Soviet Union and the United States. By the year 1948, as a consequence of the cold war, Korea was split into two sovereign states - North- and South Korea. In mid-1950 the Korean War started when North Korea attacked its brother in the south. Early on the United Nation came to the rescue of South Korea but when first UN troops crossed the 38th parallel on October 1st 1950, the Chinese sent a military intervention to stop the UN from progressing any further.

At the same time of the Korean War communist China also fought in the West to recapture the earlier lost Tibet. If you recall, Tibet was concurred by the Qing dynasty making it part of China. However, with the fall of the Qing empire Tibet regained some degree of forced independence again – driven by the colonial powers. The question if Tibet belongs to China is more difficult to answer than the question if Taiwan belongs to China, though, as Taiwan was never really separated. While historically Tibet belonged to China in the past, it was independent during the time of the Republic of China after the British demanded the separation between Tibet and China. However, this was something most of the "democratic" colonial powers did for decades without calling it military conquest but instead "spreading of civilisation" or "spreading of prosperity". The Chinese might not have a perfect legitimate claim on Tibet. But saying they would have no claim at all is also wrong. Especially when taking into account that originally it was neither Tibet nor China who initiated this. Whatever your view on this is, judging too fast in this matter might be the wrong thing to do as China only left Tibet due to the demands of the British in the first place and this most likely because the British feared China being too close to its colony in India.

In order to follow the role model of the Soviet Union in building a successful heavy industry, China decided to undergo aggressive policy changes towards industrialisation of the country. To finance this new industrialization new land reforms were introduced that would overall cost more than two million lives of landlords and land owners. This happened even before the "real" great leap forward took place. The old system of gentry landlords was replaced by a new system in which the peasants would now gain ownership of the land.

At the end of the day Mao believed that socialism would lead the country to new prosperity. In 1958, during their first five-year plan the communist party promoted the so called "Great Leap Forward" in an attempt to increase industrial production.

Soon after the decision to move most of the farm workers into steel producing jobs most of the crops rotted unharvested on the fields. And despite the fact that localized steel production turned out to be a bad decision Mao was blinded and decided to stick with his decision. This "great" leap forward failed however and cost the lives of millions of people during the period of the great Chinese famine. In China this period is known as the three years of famine (三年大饑荒). Estimates of the number of people starving to death are ranging from 15 million all the way to at least 45 million. The total number is not known, however. The total number of deaths that resulted from Mao's many political decisions are even higher, ranging from 40 to more than 70 million deaths in the country due to additional causes of death like execution and forced labour.

As a consequence of the many deaths and the worsening situation in the country, many people started to protest as they saw this as their last resort. Again, the worsening economic condition led to turmoil in the country and led to counter-movements like the great proletarian cultural revolution, better known as cultural revolution, that was launched by Mao Zedong in order to preserve communism in the country and save the country from a collapse. The goal (that he formulated) was to finally overcome capitalist elements and to make the country a strong communist state. This way China would be free from its struggles once and for all.

One important development that still took place under the rule of the communist party and Mao Zedong as their leader was the liberation of the women in the country. In contrast to previous times, women were now allowed to join the labour force which proved to be important for the overall development of the country. This early liberation meant however that women now had to bear an extra burden with working two jobs. One at home as housewife and a second in the factory.

With the catastrophic developments that were coming out of the great leap forward Mao's power diminished and Liu Shaoqi (刘少奇) and Deng Xiaoping (邓小平) took control over more and more administrative duties in the country. Mao however tried to maintain the power he had left by mobilizing young people as his "Red Guards" and motivated them to participate in the proletarian revolution. However, instead of helping the country the red guards would go and terrorize citizens and spread fear among the people. Not long after that, Mao also removed Liu and Deng[24] from their post as he saw their power growing while his diminished and regarded them as disaster-bringing capitalist. After many years of illness Mao passed away in 1976. A liberating moment for China.

Mao Zedong build up China after the second world war and while many of his decision had terrible consequences for the people he still managed to promote the status of women in the country, increase the number of literate people from 30% to more than 60% and in a way he left behind a clean slate on which Deng Xiaoping and other leaders could build a new and prosperous China.

With Deng Xiaoping as leading figure in the country from the years 1978 until his official retirement in 1989 China experienced new growth as a consequence of his market-economic reforms.

---

[24] Deng previously functioned as Finance Minister from 1953 until 1954.

Right after he gained the power over the country Deng worked on bringing new prosperity to China. Already in 1978 he started what is today known as "reform and opening-up" or 改革开放 in Chinese. I lived in Shenzhen and could see with my own eyes the prosperity these reforms brought to the country. I am convinced that if it wouldn't been for Deng Xiaoping China would not be the flourishing and thriving country it is today.

Deng's early reforms focused on de-collectivization of the countryside and the farmland. Later reforms focused on decentralization of government controls. Following the example of Singapore, Deng also favoured the development of Special Economic Zones within China in order to allow for new foreign investments into the country. Within just a few years the direction of the country changed completely.

Also taking place during the reign of Deng Xiaoping was the return of Hong Kong to China which was negotiated in 1984. Thank to Deng's diplomatic expertise the United Kingdom agreed to transfer Hong Kong back to China if its independence and political system would be guaranteed for 50 years starting from 1997.

It was also under Deng Xiaoping that in 1979 the Chinese government started its one child policy in order to control the population growth.

While the reforms of Deng Xiaoping brought new prosperity to the country they were also followed by growing corruption and nepotism. Deng favoured what he called "Socialism with Chinese characteristics". However, some young people in universities were dreaming about westernized concepts like democracy and couldn't care less about "Socialism with Chinese characteristics". In 1989 protest against the authoritarian party leadership escalated in the Tiananmen Square protest where students fought for freedom of the press, democracy and against corruption. In China this protest is often referred to as the June Fourth Incident (六四事件). Pictures went around the world in which the government sent tanks in order to stop the demonstrations. Responsible for this military intervention was then premier Li Peng

(李鹏). Li was the fourth Premier of the People's Republic of China and served from 1987 until 1998.

Even though Deng was not directly in charge of how the Tiananmen protest were handled he still retired from his public position in the same year.

However, don't be fooled by thinking that he was now out of the picture. He was keeping the control of the country in the background. Jiang Zemin (江泽民) emerged as new general secretary of the central committee of the Communist Party of China. Reforms under his rule followed Deng Xiaoping's concept of having a socialist state with Chinese characteristics. Under his rule Hong Kong also finally returned from the British in 1997 to China and just two years later Macau followed from the Portuguese. China joined the World Trade Organization (WTO) on the 11th of December 2001 and the Chinese middle class reappeared and prepared itself for the fast growth that would soon follow.

From 2002 onwards Hu Jintao (胡锦涛) followed in the big footsteps left behind him as new general secretary and leader of China. Under his rule the economy followed its earlier growth-trend and rural areas developed fast under new government policies.

During China's 18th National Communist Party Congress in 2012, Hu Jintao was replaced in his role as General Secretary of the Communist Party by Xi Jinping (习近平). Xi holds the office up until this point. During his time in power he already introduced new measures to decrease the level of corruption in the country. Furthermore, he tightened the restrictions over the civil society with methods like Internet censorship. He additionally promoted the so-called Belt and Road Initiative to maintain the growth the country experienced in earlier years.

There is much to say about Xi and his politics and recent developments but at this point it is time to close the chapter of China's past. Instead, we will now look at China's present. At its current state

China is covering more than 9.5 million square-kilometres[25]. It has 22 provinces, five autonomous regions, four direct-controlled municipalities, and two special administrative regions. China is a country of many extremes but also of beauty and fascinating facts. In order to understand China better we will look at how China differentiates itself from other countries and how different aspects are dealt with in China. Before that I want to keep a promise though and give a more in-depth look at Confucianism, Taoism, Legalism, and Buddhism and talk about the key take-aways from this section.

---

[25] That is 3.7 million square miles.

# CONFUCIANISM

儒

Let's come back to Confucius and talk more about his teachings. We already learned, that Confucius was only one of many scholars who existed during the Zhou dynasty and was still influenced by the omnipresent Shang culture. The two probably most famous scholars of Confucianism that you should know include Confucius (551 BC - 479 BC) and Mencius (372 BC - 289 BC). Funny enough, Confucius mainly managed to reach his modern fame purely because his teachings were written down and those of others were not.

In order to understand his teachings better we also have to remember, that Confucius lived during a time in which feudal lords were still ruling over the country. Also, something to bear in mind and probably not too surprising is the fact that Confucius himself was pretty much interested in being part of the upper rather than the lower class, so his teachings were mainly directed towards the ruling class of the Zhou empire.

Influenced by the existing culture, Confucius like many others still believed in the commonly-spread idea of the cult of heaven.

For Confucius the heaven which is also known as Tiān (天) was the embodiment of a system of legality in the world. Tiān can thus be understood as the natural order of things. This natural order implied that heaven follows a set universal law, rather than being independent. This law in return is called "Tao" (道) and is similar to the Tao that we have in Taoism. Tao is the underlying nature of the universe and humans should act according to this law. It is seen as a particular approach to life and includes traditions that are seen as necessary.

The main objective of Confucianism during its early days was to establish a harmonic society.

During his years of teaching, Confucius left three major virtues that he saw as the main basis of morality and as necessary to create a harmonic society.

The first one was humanity or compassion (In Chinese known as rén or 仁). The second one was ritual propriety (lǐ) or 理 in Chinese. The third one was parental respect (xiào - 孝 in Chinese). The first basis – humanity – was the empathy that humans have and their love for others. The second basis – ritual propriety – was thus a consequence of the first basis in order to show the humanity. The third basis – respect for elders – was in contrast seen as a naturally-occurring virtue.

However, there were many more concepts to Confucianism and in fact early Confucian scholars during the Han dynasty describe five important constants for Confucianism – the so called Wǔcháng (五常). The five constants are: Rén (benevolence), which you should already know, Yì (righteousness), Lǐ (proper rite), Zhì (knowledge), and Xìn (integrity). In addition to that they also describe four Confucian virtues called Sìzì (四字). The four accompanying virtues are: Zhōng (loyalty), Xiào (filial piety), another concept you should be familiar with, Jié (contingency), and Yì again.

I remember an incident where I observed parents who would come to Peking University with their two- or three-year-old children in order to study mathematics with them close to the University lake. This was surprising to me since I was used to children playing on the playground rather than doing mathematics at such an early age. This however is one (if not the most important) legacy of Confucianism on China in my opinion. In Confucianism it is believed that commitment to constant education and learning is not only important but also fundamental to life. This commitment to learning and education goes so far that someone should not be discriminated for any reason but that instead a meritocratic way is the right approach to things. This meritocracy oftentimes goes hand in hand with prosperity and economic development.

Another one of the ideas that was part of the school that Confucius followed says that the ruler should not intervene in daily policies and rather observe and offer sacrifices to establish harmony with the law. This is quite interesting as we have to remember that this ideology was adopted after the king of the Zhou lost most of his ruling power and only became a religious figurehead in the country.

Yet another idea that was wide spread during Confucius' time was that the family is at the centre of daily life with the eldest male as ruling figure. In the family itself, the son had to obey and follow the father and the wife had to obey her husband. The Confucian thought is thus teaching that the young should obey the old, but also that women should obey men. With the first still being relevant in China and the second not being part of Chinese traditions anymore. Women enjoy an equal status to men in China since the Communist took over the rule in 1949.

The state itself was seen as an extension of the original family. This makes it a bit easier to understand how the emperor (the son of heaven) was seen as superior to oneself and had thus to be obeyed. He was the father of all. Another concept, that of respecting the elders shaped China in the sense that it is custom to be loyal to authority. This, is probably also one of the factors that is contributing to the corruption and nepotism that was common amongst Chinese officials. While Confucianism makes it clear that family is very important it is a concept that today is in a fierce competition with a globalizing world. Young people are leaving their elders in the villages to work in cities like Shenzhen or go abroad for university and settle down outside of China, away from their family.

One of the important ideas described by Confucius that I want to mention was the idea, that a country should not be ruled by someone who earned this title by birthright. Instead, a leader should qualify himself through outstanding moral qualification and leadership. And in addition to that, the ruler should employ people with high moral standards as himself and then put them in key positions to guarantee the success of the country.

Despite that, throughout history Confucianism was used as an instrument to serve the interest of the gentry and ruling classes of the country. For example, Confucianism focused on how citizens should behave and what they should do for their ruler rather than the other way around. In addition to that, like mentioned earlier in this book, the selection of government officials following the Confucianism approach led to high level of corruption and nepotism in the country.

Confucius had not only inherited the ideas of his generation but also thoughts of how to reform the state and the feudal system. Additionally, Confucius talked about social order and moral teachings but his teachings did not find any fame or recognition during his time. Only more than 300 years after his death did his teachings find recognition and were adjusted to the "new" times as Confucianism helped to solve the problem of big families living together in an already densely populated country. Following his teachings, the government was faced with new unseen challenges like the (unsurprising at this point) high level of corruption and an increasing wealth gap that was present in the entire country.

Later on, during the Song dynasty the new Neo-Confucianism was heavily influenced by Buddhism. While Confucianism was held in high regards during earlier periods and the period of the Qing, its popularity would decline after this period as Communism became the new religion.

In order to survive as a country China decided to turn its back on Confucianism. During the early years of communist China, the status of Confucianism as a school of thought was declining and only under Deng Xiaoping did Confucianism find a place in China again. However, in an open and modern China the actual role of Confucianism is diminishing from day to day as it is faced with new challenges.

In contrast to Legalism, which we will talk about next, Confucianism taught that the rule of men is higher than the rule of law. This traditional and outdated view however did not have too much influence on China as the country continuously made efforts to establish a strong rule of law. The overall impact of Confucianism on the people is important to understand, however. Confucianism never existed alone in China and other concepts like Legalism, Taoism, Buddhism and Communism also left their impact on the country. While Confucianism is important to understand some Chinese characteristics, its overall impact on China however is oftentimes exaggerated. There are multiple reasons why Confucianism will still play a role for the Chinese, though. First, many but not all of the teachings are part of the ancient wisdoms that have so far been valuable for China.

Second, as China's power is growing in the world and the country is becoming more self-reliant many Chinese are proud of their traditions, including Confucianism which is one of these traditions.

We can thus conclude that while Confucianism will help us to understand China a bit better and while it will continue to have its impact on the country, other values like nationalism and globalization are competing with this old tradition for influence amongst the new generation of Chinese people. Additionally, other concepts merged with Confucianism over hundreds of years which makes it hard to split them apart. Let's still do it though and have a look at Legalism next.

# LEGALISM

# 法家

Legalism, unsurprisingly, focuses on the believe that a rule of law is necessary in order for a country to be successful. This means that it effectively puts Legalist on the other side of the spectrum compared to Confucianist. In Legalism, the ruler is seen as the natural source of all laws which makes him naturally stand above the law itself. In Confucianism on the other hand a leader should qualify himself through outstanding moral qualification and leadership. Rather than having a strong law, the morality of the people plays a more important role in Confucianism.

Over the years Legalism developed into an important concept for China due to multiple factors.

Generally, it turned out to be extremely useful for the ruling power to unify thoughts and to consolidate national strategies. In contrast to Confucianism, Legalism argues that a single law is needed that applies equally among all individuals, no matter if they are ruler or citizen, farmer or military official. One law to rule them all. While

Confucianism was one strategy that gave power to the emperor, Legalism was another possible approach that helped many rulers across the different dynasties to maintain their power.

In the Legalist school the usage of incentives and formal institutions was seen as a useful instrument to maintain the power of the ruler. In such circumstances the ruler would most of the time establish a stronger government that he would then control with even stronger incentives. He himself would be all the way at the top of the food chain.

If you remember, the famous Qin Shi Huang (秦始皇), who is today best known for his famous terracotta army, managed to unite China as a country with the help of a Legalist system. During the time of unification, the power was taken away from the former feudal lords and instead a uniform system of administration was set-up in the country. This in return avoided warfare between the different states and finally paved the way for a united China. Another legalist approach that Qin Shi Huang used was to deprive the military officials from their power and to establish a new civil governor and a third controlling official to prevent the creation of new feudal lords. This was actually nothing new but an already common tactic from followers of the Legalist school that was used in order to control powerful ministers. The Legalist were convinced that the division of power is necessary among officials in order to assure that the ruler will keep his power and can rule without disturbances. In addition to this, government officials were usually selected based on an examination system rather than nepotism.

Legalism also emphasized the importance of building institutions and administrative positions as mentioned earlier. This is what we also saw during the Qin dynasty.

If you recall, Confucianism gave a stronger authority to people with high moral standards. Legalist, however, saw it as crucial to monopolize policies in the hands of the ruler and to use rigorous protocols and control in order to hold the system together. Legalist accepted that people do not always have high moral standards and they understood for the need of a legal system that deals with this issue.

The only way for the ruler too keep his power once he established it was by keeping a tight control over his citizen and government officials. For example, the Legalist school argues that rewards and punishments should both be significant in order make policies more effective. Another way to make sure that policies were effective was by keeping the citizens poor and by restricting their free choice. This also made it easier (and less costly) to incentivise people.

We can sum up Legalism with just three tools. First, the law or Fa as it is known in Chinese, which was used to rule over the citizen. Second, political tactics (or Shu) which were necessary to guarantee a strong government on the one hand and the rule of the emperor on the other hand. Third and last was authority (or Shi). These three tools were necessary in order to maintain the authority and legitimacy of the ruler.

The Legalist school was important for the future development of China as a country because the legacy of this school left behind functioning institutions on which many future dynasties would be built. In addition to that, establishing a strong rule of law was beneficial for future growth in the country. Following and accepting a strong rule of law still plays a major part in the minds of many Chinese. The general Legalist understanding of having a strong rule of law gained new prominence under Deng Xiaoping's and Xi Jinping's rule, who both put their trust in this system. Both of them followed an early understanding of the Legalist that a strong rule of law is necessary in order for China to succeed as a country. For them however the reasons are different. Today a strong rule of law is mainly seen as beneficial in decreasing the level of corruption in a country and increasing the level of foreign direct investment. Foreign investment can be seen as a driver of the economy that helps to increase structural change. This is why we will dedicate a chapter in this book to this topic.

As you can see at this point already, modern China is not only influenced by one ideological idea but by a blend of multiple ideas instead. Confucianism, Legalist, Taoism, Buddhism all left their impact on the country.

# TAOISM

# 道教

Continuing our list we will next look at Taoism. Taoism is oftentimes also referred to as Daoism, though for the sake of consistency we will continue to refer to it as Taoism.

Lao Tzu, one of the major contributors to Taoism, is convinced that the best life is lived in harmony with the law of the universe (Tao - 道)[26]. Contrary to the view of Confucius, who focused on how people should behave in their social environment, Lao Tzu was always convinced that men should not participate in the rites and ceremonies but should rather choose a self-imposed isolation.

Taoism is in many ways a counter movement to Confucianism but also to Legalism, thus creating a triangle between the three. While Confucianism sees hierarchical organization and order as important,

---

[26] Tao can be seen as the underlying natural order of the Universe. In a way it has no essence because it is non conceptual.

Taoism is praising the simple life instead. For Taoist a good life is a simple life that is lived in harmony with the nature and that is free from the desire to achieve social ascendancy. It is in a way a great belief to keep poor people poor and stop them from thriving for power. Thus, a great tool for every ruling power to use to stop the many ambitions of the people.

One important concept in Taoism is that of "wu wei" or 無爲 in Chinese which describes and emphasizes "actions without intention". Wu wei describes a state of effortless action or action without action (wei wu wei) as some call it. It is seen as a way of life and thus as a pathway to a rich and fulfilling life.

This concept goes hand in hand with other important ideas of Taoism like compassion (慈), frugality (儉), and humility (顺). This concept and ideology is in Chinese known as 不敢為天下先 which would translate to "don't thrive to be the first in the world". The intended message here is clear: Do not thrive for power.

The idea of living in harmony with the universe goes one step further, though. In a state of selflessness, a distinction between the "I" and the "You" would disappear. A state of complete freedom from prejudices.

In a way Taoism is about passive achievement rather than active. It is therefore believed by Taoist like Lao Tzu that if there would be an active government you cannot be happy. And therefore, like explained in earlier chapters, most of the Taoist moved outside of the cities and lived on farms, to be as far away from an active government as possible. And while the Taoist tried to stay away from ambitions, the Confucianist gained more and more power in the cities and stirred the direction of China.

When putting Taoism and Confucianism in the Chinese context you could say that Confucianism was a belief for the ruling power while Taoism was one for the peasants and farmers.

# BUDDHISM

佛教

B uddhism (or Han Buddhism as it is also known in China) has shaped the Chinese culture over many years in a variety of ways. The first form of Buddhism that came to China was called Mahayana[27] Buddhism. Today it is one of the two major branches of Buddhism that exist. It can be seen as a collection of many teachings which is why you also might see many variations of Buddhism all across China and all across the world.

Despite the differences, there is still an important core set of traditions across all these variations. Therefore, I want to talk more about these core sets an believes.

In Mahayana Buddhism (from now on just referred to as Buddhism) we have the Buddha[28] as a spiritual king in the centre of everything. The general goal for Buddhists is to reach a state of Nirvana, thus following the path of the first Buddha, Siddhartha Gautama. Nirvana

---

[27] Mahayana means "Great Vehicle".
[28] Buddha means literally the enlightened one.

itself is described a state of transcendence devoid of self-reference. It is important to note that Buddhist do not belief in a god, but believe that everything is in a constant flow instead and that nothing is permanent. This also translates to life which is seen as endless, because at the end of your life you are reborn again. Since life is in a permanent flow, too, Buddhist believe that no temporary state lasts forever. Thus, there won't always be bad times and there won't always be good times.

In Buddhism there are a few common practices like the worship of the Buddhas and the Bodhisattvas (those who are on their path to Buddhahood) through different offerings or simply the worship of Devas (non-human beings who are almost godlike).

Another common practice – and one that is very common in Chinese tradition – is paying respect to the elderly during Ancestors day. This day is also known as Qing Ming festival (清明节) in China. Part of this tradition is a religious ceremony that helps the souls of the dead to find their way to the spirit world. What is interesting is that during the Zhou dynasty for example, the Chinese used smoke from burning wood in order to help the spirits to go from the human world to the spirit world. This is very typical and special for Buddhism in China because old Chinese traditions of ancestor worship merged with the Buddhist traditions that came from India to China.

A third common practice is offering compassion towards everyone and every living being. Common beliefs of Buddhist can include the belief in the existence of gods, ghost and a hell realm, which we will learn more about in a second. One important belief is that karma matters because it will impact how someone is reborn. Thus, many Buddhist believe in a so called karmic retribution (報應) where cause and effect are strictly linked together.

In order to achieve Buddhahood a set of virtues should be practiced. These virtues are known as paramitas and include: The perfection of giving, the perfection of moral conduct (or discipline), the perfection of patient endurance, the perfection of diligence, the perfection of meditation and finally the perfection of transcendent wisdom. Simple, right?

In China traditional practices go from meditation and vegetarianism all the way to mantra recitation and mindfulness. These practices became common among ordinary people in China during the Ming and other dynasties. Especially famous are the two beliefs in karma and rebirth among Chinese Buddhist. This is why we will have a further look into the four noble truths, karma, and rebirth as these are three important aspects to understand Buddhism and thus hopefully China a bit better.

The four noble truths, which are basically the essence of Buddha's teachings, focus on the suffering of life and its aspects. In substance they focus on the truth of suffering, the cause of suffering, the end of suffering, and finally the path that leads to the end of suffering. One thing that Buddha and John Maynard Keynes have in common is that they both believe that only death is certain and that we are thus all dead in the long run. However, I would assume that only one of those two believed in rebirth. The "noble truths" are intended to help with the general suffering that humanity faces and see the cause of all suffering in desire and ignorance. Capitalism and material desire are thus the cause of almost all suffering. Ignorance on the other hand means not seeing the world as it actually is, which can only lead to greed, envy, and more suffering. This suffering can only end through achieving Nirvana, a transcendent state in which one is finally free from suffering. The last truth basically says that following the Buddhist way of living life (the virtues or paramitas described earlier) can lead to Nirvana.

Buddhism further introduces the concept of Karma which ultimately concerns all the actions a person takes throughout his life - the good and the bad. Good karma essentially derives from doing good things and leads to happiness and – surprise – bad karma comes from doing bad things and leads to misery. What is good and what is bad can be very subjective though as both of these concepts are introduced by men and mostly defined by society.

Karma becomes important when we take into account the so called "cycle of birth". As you already know, Buddhist believe that a human will be reborn once he dies (assuming he does not reach Nirvana).

People who accumulated a lot of positive karma will be reborn in one of three positive realms and people who accumulated bad karma will be reborn in one of three bad realms. The highest realm is actually not that of the god but that of mankind itself, because man are free from the relentless conflicts that gods and demigods have, and it offers the only opportunity to achieve Nirvana. The three bad realms are those of animals, ghost and finally hell.

As you can probably see at this point if not earlier, Buddhism shows some similarities with Taoism and favours a minimalistic lifestyle over one of greed and desire.

Buddhism actually gained a lot of influence during some early dynasties but lost most of its earlier favour over the years. Only since Deng's reform and opening up policy did Buddhism find new soil in China. Buddhist temples all across the country were restored and since enjoyed the status of great tourism spots. The Chinese State Administration for Religious Affairs, however, keeps a close eye on many Buddhist temples and makes sure that they don't turn too much into commercial businesses. Unfortunately, I can't tell you if the Chinese State Administration for Religious Affairs is successful or not and I do not indent to talk about their success at this point as there are more interesting things to talk about. Despite Buddhism losing influence in China we can see some works that were strongly impacted by Buddhist culture. One of these works is "Journey to the West" (or "Monkey King" which is also known as 西遊記 or Xī Yóu Jì in Chinese) – a book I wish I had read as a child. Journey to the West counts as one of four great works of Chinese literary history[29]. The story is about a monk (Xuanzang or 玄奘) who went to search for Buddhist scripts. A monkey who was raised by heaven follows Xuanzang on his adventure and uses his unique and magical talents to defeat the many monsters on the way and overcome the challenges the hero has to face. At the end, they manage to bring back the scripts to

---

[29] The other three are, The Three Kingdoms, The Water Margin and The Dream of the Read Chamber.

the emperor of the Tang dynasty and thus attain Buddhahood on the way on account of their trials and self-cultivation.

While the book beautifully illustrates how the Monkey became Sun Wukong (孫悟空) thanks to overcoming his struggles and trials, many families in China struggle to let their children face a similar trial in life.

# LESSONS LEARNED

Before starting to look at China today we should take a moment and think about what we have learned from China's history so far. Analysing the past and interpreting it will turn out to be useful when we will start to look at the different aspects of daily life in China. Hopefully, it will also come quite handy once we will look at China's future.

Of course, different people have different opinions. In this section I will focus on my own opinion which may or may not be aligned with the opinion of others. Due to the fact that I will make my own interpretations I want to encourage you to make your own judgement as well and decide for yourself if you want to agree or disagree with me. I will summarize the conclusions that we can draw from China's history in form of a list of six lessons. This list is far from complete and you can think about additional lessons that we can learn from China's history and add them to your own personal list.

# THE CENTRE

———

L ooking back at China's history, we see that over the thousands of years many dynasties came, ruled, and left again. Some of these dynasties focused on war with its surrounding countries, others focused on developing the country as such. In reality, most were kept busy on both fronts - while China was covered with chaos and turmoil it was also big enough to give enough freedom to developments.

What we can learn from the many years of history, though, is that China is at its strongest when the country has a strong core. In contrast to this, China is weakest when the centre of the country is weak and China has no clear red line it can follow.

You can easily observe, that during the early years of China none of the existing feudal states had enough power or control to strive on its own. Only once alliances were formed and a stronger centre emerged, can we observe the creation of new promising trade routes and growing prosperity in the country. With the unification of the feudal states came a corresponding unification of the language as China was then able to focus on internal development.

If you remember, Qin Shi Huang, the emperor of the Qin dynasty, died in 210 BC on one of his later travels after contracting a sickness. The death of the emperor led a disastrous rebellion and a change in power because the country was left without a strong centre and without a guiding hand. By 206 BC the Han dynasty emerged after many years of turmoil and would remain the ruling dynasty for the next 400 years to come because it again profited from a strong centre that allowed for crucial developments in the country.

When we look at the dynasties of the Jin or Ming we can see many different developments happening, ranging from philosophical to economical.

In addition to that, during the times in which China had a strong centre, China moved towards a more united country, which led to even more prosperity and power. In contrast to that, divided periods like the period of the five dynasties or northern and southern dynasties were usually characterized with warfare, turmoil, and death. These transition periods brought instability to the Country and left China weak and vulnerable to foreign invasion. If we look back to the years 907 until 960 AD, the period of the five dynasties, we can see another dynasty ending through assassination and a period of transition in which China is in turmoil and characterised with relative instability. What was missing during these periods was a strong centre, that on the one hand helped to unite the country and hold it together and on the other helped to boost economic development and prosperity.

Without a clear line - a clear centre - China is weak. With a strong centre, in contrast, China is strong and prosperous. When looking at present day China we can see how the current ruling party in Beijing understands these dynamics and thus tries to keep the country in a close grip to ensure that it stays on the right track. I'm on Deng Xiaoping's side here and think that China needs to open up and develop democratic institutions further to be successful in the long-run. This however does not mean that China should become a democracy. This is something we should talk about in the third chapter, though.

# MODERNIZATION

二

Modernization is crucial for many things and we can argue that it is also crucial to the development of China. Many dynasties had to learn their lesson when they failed to modernize and lost the control over the country as a consequence.

One of the best examples of this was the Qing dynasty, which constantly struggled to modernize and in the end, watched more develop nations humiliate the country. During the time of the Qing, from the nineteenth century onwards, more and more industrial goods were finding its way into the country. They were brought by the colonial powers, amongst others, and ultimately prevented a period of early industrialization in China since there was no need for innovation. The Qing dynasty saw growth until the middle of the eighteenth century, but it started to decline soon after.

Additionally, the Qing dynasty was struggling with a never-ending increase in its population which grew over the years almost exponentially to an enormous size. While this helped to compensate for technical innovation it in the end caused more problems than it solved. Consequently, the Qing could not modernize the country fast enough in order to keep food production growing at the same pace as the population.

Another reason for the decline of the Qing was that the gentry remained anti-industrial and anti-capitalism for too long. They tried to operate necessary enterprises such as mining, melting, porcelain production as long as possible as classical government establishments rather than private enterprises. This went so far that the gentry favoured the investments in land rather than in industries per se. The fear was that these private enterprises could at any moment be taken away by the government, controlled by the officials or forced to be sold at set prices. These prices were oftentimes set by corrupt and dishonest officials. As a consequence, a typical businessman only felt secure when he had first invested in land, or when he succeeded to establish a strong connection with government officials that protected him as long as he maintained good relationships.

No doubt, despite all of this, Chinese businesses and industries kept on developing, but China did not develop at a speed that allowed for transformation of the country from an agricultural focused country into a modern industrial nation like we saw happening in the west.

Once the United Kingdom showed up at the doorsteps of China the decline of the country began to accelerate with new conflicts arising. China reached an all-time low in its speed of development after the two opium wars with Britain and saw itself overrun and trampled on.

The period of the late Qing marks a devastating time in Chinese history. The country lacked crucial developments reaching from a modern army to an improved agricultural production. As the situation became more severe people gradually realized that things needed to change in order for China to maintain its importance in the world. These developments lead to turmoil in the country as we have seen many times before. We saw the Qing dynasty ending under the increasing threat from outside and the numerous failures at home brought even further escalating instability. China suffered extremely from these developments. However, I do believe that China learned from its history and now – maybe just out of fear - spends skyrocketing sums of money on research and development in order to be at the forefront of future markets. These investments seem to pay off so far and China is leading innovation in many different areas from robotics to machine learning.

China, a nation of 1.4 billion people, strongly depends on a continuous modernization of the country in order to maintain and grow its dominance in Asia and the world. And more crucially, in order to bring prosperity to its citizens.

# BORDERLANDS

三

China, together with Russia, has the largest number of land borders with neighbouring countries in the world. Fourteen in total to be precise. They are (Running anti-clockwise from the East to the West) North Korea, Russia, Mongolia, Kazakhstan, Kyrgyzstan, Tajikistan, Afghanistan, Pakistan, India, Nepal, Bhutan, Myanmar, Laos and Vietnam. In addition to that, the East and South China Sea are bounded on the west by Vietnam and on the east by the Philippines and Japan, South Korea and Taiwan, which at the end of the day leads to additional border conflicts.

China however is used to sharing its borders with many diverse and different countries for thousands of years already and learned its lessons from it – by now, China knows very well how to deal with foreign countries and how to capitalise on its position.

While China has a vast number of neighbouring countries, China wasn't always the big country it is now and there were days when China was smaller with less neighbours surrounding it. Looking at the history of China we saw the face of the country change with almost every change in the ruling power.

Going one step further than just looking at China's borders we can see that the number of border conflicts seems countless. We have already learned that by the year 1876 the Japanese started to penetrate far into the Korean peninsula, which at that time was still under Chinese protection. Furthermore, during the time of the Song dynasty China was split into multiple parts and saw conflicts between the above-mentioned Song, the Jurchen Jin and the Liao dynasty.

China was also split apart during the time of the Northern and Southern dynasties, the period of the ten kingdoms and many other periods in China's long history.

China saw border conflicts coming and going all the time. At some point in history China and Russia were in conflict over Mongolia. In 1911 Russian interest dominated in the outer Mongolia region which led to the so-called Russo-Chinese treaty signed in 1913, in which outer Mongolia was recognized as an independent state and Inner Mongolia would remain a part of the Chinese realm. In addition to that, with the outbreak of the first world war, the Japanese increased their already dominating influence in the region. This was by far not the only conflict and we can see the price that China has to pay for its size. There have been conflicts between China and Myanmar; China and India; China and Tibet, the Philippines, Malaysia and so on. Many of them still exist.

China however also learned from many of its disputes and as a consequence shares many friendly borders with its neighbours today wherever it can.

China shares its second longest border with Russia. There are some disputes between these two countries due to earlier treaties signed by the Qing empire and Russia. Additional disputes took place in China's Xinjiang Uyghur autonomous region (XUAR). However, currently both sides now refer to each other as strategic partners, which seems undoubtedly driven by Beijing and its interest in the region.

China's longest border is with a country you would have probably not guessed right away, which is Mongolia. Mongolia once ruled over most of China during the Yuan dynasty. Now the power dynamic between these two countries has changed. However, China is still reliant on Mongolia as a strategic partner and increasingly turns to them to meet its energy needs.

Currently, China's Xinjiang province in the far northwest of the country shares a border with Kazakhstan and there exists a close relationship with Kazakhstan which serves China's long-term interests in the region[30]. As you can see however, Xinjiang is strategically extremely important to China which is why China is working hard at integrating the region further into the communist system.

One of the more difficult border conflicts is that with India. On a first glance it seems that India and China should get along well, since they are mostly cut-off from each other through the Himalayas. And indeed, the borders between the India and China have been peaceful for thousands of years.

This changed however once the British decided to put their finger into the pie. Most of the disputes are about strategically important regions like "Aksai Chin", which connects Tibet with the western province of Xinjiang. Another dispute is over "Arunachal Pradesh" which China sees as geographically and culturally being part of Tibet – which plays an important part in China's border conflicts. The problem is that both of these regions are of utmost importance to China's security and development in the west. Up until today China and India have not managed to negotiate an agreement regarding these two areas.

Another country to talk about is Myanmar. Myanmar has a long history of conflicts with China. Only since China started supporting the military dictatorship in Myanmar in 1986, did the conflicts come to an end. Today Myanmar is highly dependent on the Chinese financially

---

[30] The strong cooperation between Kazakhstan and China comes with many benefits. Not only does China profit from the existing oil fields but having Kazakhstan as a strategic partner helps to prevent Uighur separatism in the west. In fact, China is working hard with its western partners like Tajikistan, Kazakhstan, and Afghanistan to fight Islamic fundamentalism.

and militarily. On the flipside, Myanmar is currently delivering oil, gas and other natural resources to China.

There were also historically multiple tensions with China and Vietnam, the most recent being over the Spratly Island, which is an oil rich area in the South China Sea – but again it's best to talk more in depth about the South China Sea in a separate chapter as this is a long and more complex topic just by itself.

The biggest disputes however is probably with none of China's bordering countries but with the US instead. Currently the US is still military active in Asia to uphold its position as self-proclaimed "world power".

As you can see by this few examples, China is used to border disputes for thousands of years and is still struggling with many disputes. The last two hundred years alone make up for enough disputes to write multiple books. China has learned to deal with its neighbouring countries though and found a way to successfully resolve disputes and create win-win situations. In addition to that, China knows its increasingly important role in the world and has gained confidence that followed from Deng's opening up reform. Currently the border with India remains unresolved. China however has a strong military presence at its borders and can live with an "unsolved" scenario for many of the conflicts, because it will still be enough to keep the Americans at a distance.

China has also learned from the many years of occupation from the British and Japanese and is making sure that something similar will not happen in the next century. Initiatives like the Belt and Road Initiative give China a strong advantage that both the British and Japanese were missing. It makes other countries more dependent on China.

I am convinced that neither China nor its neighbouring countries are interested in an armed conflict. Instead, a power demonstration will be enough to make the US retrieve further away over time and protect the Chinese realm. China will follow its path and work on building economic ties with neighbouring countries rather than attacking them. In the past, trade and economic ties proved to be the best alternative for diplomacy in Asia which proved particularly successful for China during the Tang and Ming dynasty. As we have seen over the last years, China learned from its earlier mistakes and found working alternatives to hostile occupation.

# THE EMPIRE

四

C hina was an empire for thousands of years and saw hundreds of emperors coming and going.

Only after the British arrived with their strong naval fleet in the south did China see it as necessary to adjust the country to western concepts and to end its long running empire.

Having a ruling emperor was in the mindset of the Chinese for decades, though. One of the biggest changes that the country faced after the end of the Qing dynasty was that it was left without an emperor and had to take charge of itself now. The cliques, who previously always tried to influence the emperor, saw themselves without a clear objective. On the other side, military officials and the governors gained in power.

Oftentimes it was the emperor who created a strong centre in the country and who allowed for prosperity and growth to take place. It was under the rule of a strong emperor for example that the feudal states reunited and that the language was unified. This was a crucial development for China's success and it would have not happened like this under a democratic rule.

What we have to learn and understand though is that China has changed over thousands of years, with new borders emerging after almost every change in dynasty. Thus, it is not too surprising, that one Chinese empire is not like another. So, the question here is how history and the different empires influence the Chinese thought, behaviour and overall position today.

One thing is certain and that is that the Chinese understand that their prosperity comes from having a strong centre that has the interest of the country as a main priority. China was used to having an emperor for a long time and many of the most crucial developments for China's success happened during the rule of an emperor. In fact, many times, China's emperors created a necessary stability in which economic growth could take place. Thus, it is not too surprising that the Chinese elite, while it understands the western approach, does not see it as necessary to lead the country as a democracy. In fact, leading the country as a democracy could turn out to be disastrous for China, its citizens, and even far away trade partners because new uncertainties could spread and slow down the development and progress of the country.

I am personally convinced, that China would not be able to succeed (the same way it does now) if it would be a democratic country. Applying western concepts to a country like China could lead to even higher levels of corruption, poverty, and turmoil. Communism works, because it borrows many elements from the old empires. However, don't get me wrong, there are many things that are wrong with communism in my opinion and there are many benefits of democracy, too. I myself grew up in a democratic and liberal country and would not want trade that experience.

Despite this, it is hard to generalise and assume that applying democracy to China would bring success as China's roots lie somewhere else. It is important to understand that while the answer may not be democracy, a strong legal system and working institutions are needed to stabilise the country and remove the risk of a dictator overstepping boundaries.

We talked about China's necessity to have a strong centre not long ago. This is something that is also valued by many Chinese who remember the prosperous developments under old and long gone dynasties with a strong centre, but can still value the current developments that follow the strong and unified leadership of the Chinese Communist Party (CCP).

We also talked about China's countless number of border conflicts and learned about the many years of humiliation that China experienced from the British and the Japanese. These two things make people look back at the different empires and wish for a similar strong power in the centre that will protect the interest of the country.

In the end, what we can take away is that China is not only used to being an empire but that it also values the many advantages that came along with it. The strong centre being by far the most important. Of course, the Chinese are aware of the downsides that come along with it, too. Many emperors (especially in the end) only served as puppets to more powerful cliques operating in the back. Nowadays, we can see how free press and freedom of thought are in danger in China, again.

At the end, all this helped to establish a working communist government that learned from the lessons of the past. In a way what Deng Xiaoping said proves to be very true and China is indeed a socialist country with Chinese characteristics. And Deng's approach to it, leading China to a more open, liberal country with communist characteristics in the centre seems to be the most reasonable approach going forward.

# TURMOIL

五

We cannot talk about the multiple empires that ruled over China without looking closer at the many periods of turmoil and uprisings that ended most of them. This is something that is not particularly unique to China. However, the many uprisings are important to keep in mind when looking at modern day-to-day politics in China and the lessons the Communist party learned from the early dynasties.

The risings happened without clear patterns other than that most of the times the situation for many citizens was bad. Almost every dynasty had to deal with at least one internal conflict that emerged. Many times, it was the peasants who started these revolts and who attacked the towns with its officials, moneylenders and landowners out of their frustration.

If we look back, we can see how many of these revolutions happened during times when China's centre was weak and thus failed to bring prosperity to its citizen. After the early Zhou dynasty, we observe for example how the country was faced with turmoil and instability once it lost its strong centre.

Since we already had a close look at China with a strong centre compared to a China with a weak centre, we will not spend more time on this. Instead, we will look at the risings and revolts that are characteristic for many periods in China's history and their cause and effect.

Oftentimes China lost many of its cultural achievements during the uprisings and chaos in the country which makes for a bitter period of the development of the nation, culture and innovation as such. These uprisings also continued into the modern age with many happening during the period of the Republic of China and some under the People's Republic of China.

The causes for the uprisings can differ throughout history. Sometimes, a simple draught can be enough to cause a fundamental change in the society. A common factor might not always exist, and class struggle is not always the trigger of turmoil in the country, though it is a common one. Major causes can be political change in the country as we saw many times in China's history or conflicts that emerged after new ideologies found its way into the minds of the people. Class struggle might be an underlying factor that helps to trigger the risings and the unrest. In addition to that, it is likely that class struggle will emerge out of other problems because the peasants will most likely be the one impacted the most by radical changes.

For many Chinese, domestic unrest is closely associated with the destructions imposed on China by the imperialist powers (especially Britain and Japan). Thus, many people remain fearful of political and social chaos that they experienced in the mid-19$^{th}$ century.

We can keep the conclusion short at this point. Turmoil and unrest characterized many dynasties in China's history. It caused political change and unrest in the country, destroyed cultural achievements and sent China's economic advancement back to zero. It is a scenario that is feared by many and the Chinese Communist Party (CCP) is aware of the many negative impacts that come with political uprisings in the country. The CCP is trying to keep the country stable by having a tight grip on everything that could cause turmoil. For example, the ban of many social media platforms after an uprising in China's west.

China is thus moving into a more hands-on country when it comes to oppressing protest. The CCP (as many other political parties around the world) has one major fear. Losing its power over the country. To understand this better, we will have a closer look at recent developments it in the third part of this book.

# PHILOSOPHY

六

As China's power is growing in the world and the country is becoming more self-reliant many Chinese are proud of their traditions, including Confucianism, Taoism, Buddhism to name a few.

In fact, since Deng Xiaoping's reform of opening up communist China started to show appreciation for the many beliefs that exist within the country and now sees it as one of China's many strengths. Of course, other modern values like nationalism and globalization and even communism are competing with this old tradition for influence, but the impact that these traditions have on the country will stay and only change slowly over many generations to come.

Earlier in this book we looked at the different beliefs that left their impact on China and how each of these beliefs is different from another. Confucianism for example favoured a meritocratic society while in Buddhism and Taoism abstinence was seen as favourable. Buddhism, we learned, shares some similarities with Taoism and favours a minimalistic lifestyle over one with greed and desire. We have also seen how many of the Taoist moved outside of the cities and lived a simple life, while the Confucianist gained more and more power in the cities. When putting Taoism and Confucianism in the Chinese context you could say that Confucianism was a belief for the ruling power while Taoism was one for the peasants and farmers.

Modern day China is not only influenced by one ideological idea but by a blend of multiple.

Confucianism, Legalist, Taoism, Buddhism and also Hinduism all left an impact on the country and its citizens. Many of these traditions turned out to be beneficial for China. Confucianism which favoured hard work and a mediocratic mindset while the Legalist school of thought created a strong rule of law in the country. China can be – and now finally is – proud of these beliefs. It is a belief system that formed the general basis of the Chinese society and its governance for many centuries.

Despite all this, the country became atheist (or rather communist) in 1949, once the Communist came to power and only state-monitored religious practices were allowed. As mentioned earlier, it was only under Deng Xiaoping that the Chinese view on its many beliefs changed. And while now about one-half of people claim that they don't have a religion, they are still influenced by the many years that China had a vast number of beliefs and philosophical practices.

All that being said, what we can take away is the following: When we look at China, we should not only look at it with one lens as there is no "one China". In fact, China is a country with lots of opposites. With many beliefs and schools of thought. China profited from its colourful past and the many traditions. In a way of perfect balance, the numerous philosophical traditions and beliefs created a place for everyone, some of the smartest scholars, and a thriving country.

# Second Part

## The Present of China

# PAST TO PRESENT TENSE

We have reached the present. By know you should have a general understanding of China's long and diverse history and the many aspects that shaped this fascinating country over many hundreds of years. At this point you should also be more familiar with concepts like Confucianism and Taoism. In the next part we will apply the knowledge we have gained for the first time. For this, we will first look at the key lessons that we can learn from China's history and in a next step we will look at different aspects of daily-life in China and see how these aspects work in this eastern empire. For example, we will look at things like Transportation and how it is working in China, how Family "works" in China or how life in general looks like for a typical Chinese person. You will learn and see how Confucianism left its impact on family traditions and how today the Hukou system impacts the life of many. The aim of this part is to show you the differences between life in China and life in western countries like Europe or America.

I am convinced that there is a western bias against China that is led by America. However, I believe that one reason is the missing education about this Country. The west only sees China through a keyhole and is just not seeing all of it. I thus hope, that this part will help you to get a better understanding of China.

## ABOUT THIS PART

This part will introduce modern concepts ranging from family obligation, to urbanization and gratuity in China. The aim of this part is to show what China looks like today and help you to spot differences to your own culture. I for my part grew up in Germany. However, I am sure you do not have to grow up in a western world to see differences and similarities between China and your country. In this part I will strongly rely on my own observations, academic research, and implications that we made in the first part of this book.

# FAMILY IN CHINA

The first aspect we will look at in this part of the book is Family in China. We have learned earlier that the Confucianism school emphasizes family values and personal relations. We will now have a look at modern family values and the concept of family obligation in China.

Family obligation can be seen as a collection of personal characteristics and a person's behaviour that is related to the support and respect towards family members. In the sense of family obligation, the family is seen as a big collective and a person belongs to this group and thus has responsibilities to contribute their part to the overall success (and survival) of this group. For example when an important decision has to be made it is common to take into account the needs of the family first.

If you recall, we learned that early on the role of the family was important in Chinese society and this construct still existed up until today. Furthermore, Confucianism and Buddhism both emphasised the obligation a child has towards its family and the elders. In addition to that, the fact that most of China's population was living in rural areas not too long ago contributed to a strong family feeling and a strong feeling of community belonging.

The idea of family obligation goes so far that it is common in China that children see it as important (and oftentimes even necessary) to repay their parents for being raised and taken care off in their childhood. They contribute most of their life to paying back this debt. This, while still being important in western societies is less common. I for myself, while loving my parents, never felt any obligation in paying them back for all the time and commitment they gave me during my youth.

Up until today the historical influences are relevant and modern Chinese families still emphasize the concept of family obligation while bringing up their children. Additionally, most of the classical literature taught at school puts emphasis on the value of family.

While many times the move to a more liberal and capitalist society leads to less family-oriented behaviour saying that this is also happening in China after its opening-up policy is not that easily done. While more and more people get educated outside of China and try to profit from the free-market economy many people in China still feel a strong family obligation. Thus, while family obligation might indeed decline over the years it is likely to still be of significance going forward.

One factor contributing to the fact that family obligation is still of importance is the fact that even now many people still live in rural parts of China and only selected cities (Shenzhen, Shanghai, etc.) opened up to a more capitalist approach. Those families that are left behind in the rural areas barely see any difference in their daily life and are thus less influenced by reforms like Deng Xiaoping's opening up.

In the cities many people profit from social welfare systems that are in place like healthcare and pensions (In the next part we will talk more about one famous system - the hukou system - and see how it actually works). The lack of these welfare systems in rural areas makes the concept of family obligation way more important in the rural parts of the country than in the urban areas since people are more dependent on their families.

It is still yet unclear whether this trend will continue or if it will change over the next decades. One thing that already changed however is China's one child policy - another important aspect when talking about family in China. A change in this policy that took effect on January 1st 2016 allowed Chinese couples to have two children after a decade of one-child policy in China. However, the impacts of the former policy were already visible by then. To understand them better, let's take a step back.

The initial decision to create a one-child system in which - surprise - the number of children was limited to one per couple was formed in 1979 as an initial response to the massive demographic growth in the country. The immense rise in population caused a fear of worsening economic and living conditions in China's future and caused many crowded cities to lose control over their public infrastructure and social systems.

The policy was implemented using economic incentives for young couples with one child and penalties for those who were not following the rules. These penalties were severe and included higher taxes, fines and additional disadvantages that made it almost impossible for an average family to afford a second child. Adding to this was an increased social pressure on women to only give birth to one child and those who didn't follow were frowned upon.

It is easy to see how this new system contradicts the long existing Confucian mindset in which young people are needed to support the elderly. This, however, was nothing the political decision makers considered at the time they made the decision to implement this policy.

It is estimated that with the one-child policy in place more than 300 million births were prevented. The reactions about this outcome are different and range from thankful, since it allowed to maintain a satisfactory standard of living all the way to disastrous, because it limited the freedom of choice of individuals severely[31].

The result of the policy is easily visible when visiting China. It is even more visible though, when looking at some basic statistics. In Beijing, the current capital of China, around 2/3 of the families only have one child.

While the initial goal of the one-child policy was reached and the policy was seen as satisfactory by party leaders, the outcome also comes with new problems that now need to be addressed.

One outcome is that the sex ratio between male and female drastically shifted from around 1[32] to approximately 1.2 and even 1.5 in some regions. This means there are proportionally more men than women. A development that is very visible in many parts of the country and that brings new challenges with it.

One major reason for this shift is the traditional preference for the son over the daughter, which grew out of China's history and culture. "Only a son can traditionally ensure a continuing income stream to support the family. Only a son can carry on the family line". This wish for a male heir and the strict government enforcement of the policy led to more than 14 million abortions and more than 20 million female sterilizations in 1983 alone, a year where only 21 million births were registered.

Another problem that followed as a consequence of the one-child policy is the increasing proportion of old people in China. An aging population was a problem for many industrialised countries for a long time already – China can now be added to this list. It is estimated that China's elderly population will grow with around 3% per year. By 2030 more than 25% of the population are estimated to be over 65[33]. By 2050 the numbers look even worse. While the reduction in birth rate

---

[31] I think you can easily guess which of these two views is dominant in mainland China and which is often the foreign view on the one-child policy.

[32] This means the ratio between male and female is almost equal.

[33] If this isn't troublesome enough, China is currently missing a working pension system with currently only about 20% of the elderly having some sort of pension. The rest is still relying on the support of their children.

is one reason, the increasing longevity of the population is another. Consequentially, this will lead to a disproportion between the number of people that need to be supported and those who are responsible for the support. The latter will carry a bigger burden on their shoulders.

Just as an example: A regular couple of two only children may need to support their own child(ren) and additionally four parents, as well as up to eight grandparents, without the help of any sibling or pension system. Just seeing this makes it obvious that the burden on these children is enormous and oftentimes too much for those that are only used to being in the center of the attention and taken care off.

As a consequence of these events, starting on January 1st 2016 Chinese couples were again allowed to have more than one child. This marks the official end to a policy that has restricted the life of many families for 35 years. Additionally, from 2016 onwards couples no longer needed to seek approval from the government but only need to register the birth.

However, the country had low fertility rates for years now which is the result of personal choice rather than the effect of policies. Raising a child is an expensive adventure and many Chinese families can only bear the financial burden of raising one child. Considering all the other burdens they have to carry this seems quite reasonable. Even after 2016 nothing much changed, and the birth rate stayed at a very low level with many families still only giving birth to one child. Thus, the low fertility rate is more the result of choice than of policy restrictions. As a consequence, it is unlikely that birth rates in China will see a significant increase in the upcoming years as the pressure and additional burden is unlikely to change.

# LIFE IN CHINA

# 生活

I have to admit, the topic "Life in China" is very broad and can be understood in many different ways. This is why I want to use this chapter to talk about more general concepts, one of them being the famous hukou system.

To understand the current hukou system we have to go back in time again to the early 1950s. The first kind of hukou system was implemented in Chinese cities around 1951 with the officially stated purpose of maintaining social peace and order, safeguarding people's security, and protecting their freedom of residence and movement. This system effectively gave the necessary freedom to the citizens to boost the economy. At the same time the country transformed its company structure from private and capitalist ownership to state and collective ownership in almost all areas in the years 1953 until 1956 following the communist idealism.

In those early years after the Communist took over the control of the country, the new code of laws and the regulations that were created were now aimed to differentiate residential groups to better control population movement within the country.

The 1955 version of the hukou system was first implemented with the aim to restrict urbanization and to prevent peasants from moving to the cities, which kept growing to enormous and unmanageable sizes. Cities promised jobs and the chance of a better life while many towns on the countryside could not make such promises. Thus, the calculation was easy, stay in your village and suffer from worsening economic conditions or go to the city and try to climb up the social ladder. An easy calculation for many, which led to the uncontrollable growth of many urban areas[34]. In a way, the hukou system defines the city - countryside relationship and plays an important role in shaping the society in China. One thing is sure - as a population control mechanism the hukou system shaped China's countryside from the mid-1950s onwards in a drastic way.

Part of this system was the official registration of citizenship, identity and official status which was also part of the initial objective of the system. The 1955 directive marked the shift from a registration system to more explicit government policies that were aimed at preventing unplanned population movement. In addition to that, the hukou system defines who can get employment, go to school, marry and even buy property, which was a great way for the communist party to tighten its grip on China's citizens. For example, without official approval, migrants were not able to obtain housing.

The system itself proved to be necessary, because it helped the state to work efficiently. Furthermore, the hukou system was also considered to be a necessary component of the centrally planned economy. What you have to consider is that the state budget needs to be spent on housing, food and water supply, transportation, medical facilities, schools and police stations. In order to do this, the state needs to account for the number of citizens and additionally control the number of citizens living in cities. The picture looks different in

---

[34] While time passed and many things changed it seems like this is one thing that did not change over the years as the same promise seems to hold in today's China.

rural areas however where most of these provisions are missing. More about that later, though.

The system itself originated from the already existing family registration system, which linked each family to the respective state. It emerged as a necessary response to the already existing extreme population density and labour surplus in cities.

Remember, back in the early days of the Communist regime, most of the people mainly worked in agriculture. One of the early problems of the hukou system – and one that still exist – is that cities are consistently favoured over rural areas due to the opportunity for better welfare. The hukou system consistently prevented people from emigrating to urban areas by associating them to their village or city of birth, making it even harder for many citizens to move up the social ladder. In addition to that, once implemented the system encouraged many workers to return to their rural areas, leaving the city for good.

One of the most important factors to the "success" of the hukou system is that the state had finally an absolute control over urban employment. In fact, the responsible state labour bureau is in some cases only authorized to allocate jobs to local city residents. In other cases, the recruitment by state-owned enterprises was the main channel for peasants to obtain an urban hukou during the 1960s and 1970s before Deng's game-changing reform.

By 1960 the hukou system consisted of three interdependent functions. It was the first time in China's history that people were "fixed" to their birthplace[35]. In addition to that, the Chinese state established two hierarchies. One for the cities and one for the countryside. And at this point it is to nobody's surprise that the city was privileged over the rural areas. While the city population enjoyed many benefits most of the people living on the countryside saw themselves stuck in the lowest end of society. During the great leap forward, which we briefly talked about during the history of the People's Republic of China, it was these people who suffered from the

---

[35] The only exemption from this was made for women, who were not fixed to their birthplace but rather to the location of their husband.

consequences, not the people in the cities. Systematically, all rural surplus produced was transferred to the cities. They hukou system, was and still is the major driver and cause for the deep divide between urban and rural areas that existed for many years.

While the population movement between rural areas and cities accelerated once Deng Xiaoping took over, the hukou system nevertheless continues to differentiate the population from the countryside with that from the cities. The hierarchical difference still exists up until today. Under Deng Xiaoping the population movement between rural and urban areas increased. A generally more liberal hukou policy has been adopted by the state, but China still has a long way to go. By this time,spiech around 236 million people in China are migrant workers, according to government statistics.

One of the major changes that took place under Deng's rule was the introduction of temporary residential permits and so-called blue cards, similar to the American green cards. The blue card allows its holder to invest in cities, to buy property and to receive local benefits similar to citizens. Getting a blue card is not easy though and encourages movements between already urban population to other cities rather than from rural areas to cities as money played a major role in obtaining these blue cards. The problem is a one-time fee that many cannot afford. It can vary from thousands to tens of thousands of yuan for more attractive cities like Beijing and Shanghai. However, a direct purchase of an urban hukou has recently become possible and is a great way for newly rich Chinese to obtain social welfare and access to property.

When I lived in Beijing, I saw with my own eyes how the system divides the population, even within the cities. Many people still move to the cities in order to earn a living and find a job. However, they oftentimes miss out on social benefits, free schooling and the chance to buy property. Effectively, they work to get food in their mouth and send home whatever is left. They work in the cities to make some money, but they will never be able to settle down and have a life there. For now, they are stuck with living from day to day, hoping they at least make enough money to support their grandparents and children at home, wishing that maybe their children will have a better life. The children, since they don't have the chance to get educated in the cities, stay behind and get raised by the grandparents, rather than their parents. And while recent changes allow for non-hukou holders to attend schools in urban areas, the fees and tuition still make it an impossible scenario for many low-income workers. Chinese New Year is one of the few, if not the only occasion when the parents can see their children.

The growing inequality between income, subsidies and welfare leaves no other opportunities to the people. The hukou system effectively tied China's rural population to land they do not own and could not leave. An almost unescapable scenario.

Recently there have been attempts to reform the hukou system, but I am convinced that nothing much will change as the system helps the Communist party in achieving other strategies.

However, the increasing disparity between urban and rural areas in terms of income and opportunity makes it necessary to at least further reform the system. Deng Xiaoping already weakened the migration control characteristic of the earlier hukou system, but the disparities remained. Up until today the hukou system is discriminating against rural population in many ways. The rural population are still missing out on quality education and better opportunities to climb up the social ladder. And while the hukou system helps to control the inflow into the cities and plays an important role for China to control important social and economic outcomes, the side effects of the hukou system leave a bitter taste. The implications of the system go so far that today's graduates from the best universities in the country are willing to give up well-paying jobs in order to obtain urban hukous in major cities on China's eastern and southern coast. Everything to allow their children to receive a better education and obtain a higher standard of living one day. It all seems written in the stars.

# URBANIZATION

# 城市化

We talked about the hukou system in the previous chapter, a concept that restricted urbanization for many years. In addition to that, in order to understand China a bit more, we should have a deeper look at urbanization itself and see how it looks like in today's China. In the following chapter, we will talk about transportation as one part of the urbanization strategy.

Following Deng Xiaoping's opening up reform China saw growth in its economy for the last decade and the gross domestic product (GDP) of the country grew with almost double digits for most of this period.

One effect of this swift growth was the increase in people's living standards along the east coast of the country and many urban areas in the central areas of mainland China. Following the increasing living standards and the rise in wages was a naturally increased demand for more (affordable) housing in urban areas. This is and was happening all over the world, even in most western countries, once the standard of living increased by enough. The difference for China is on the one side the double-digit growth of the economy and on the other side the enormous size and growth of the population. Both of these factors led to an unhealthy growth in demand that was hard to match with supply. Over the years house prices grew rapidly which made it almost impossible and unaffordable for the majority of the population to buy their own property. The developments of the Chinese housing market showed similarities with those of America and Europe during their respective housing bubbles. Cities like Shenzhen and Shanghai are amongst the most expensive cities in China and all over the world to buy property and only Hong Kong might be slightly more expensive.

Beijing is aware of the reality that the level of house prices is unsustainable in the long-run and that changes are needed. In fact, many are already implemented and some will still follow to keep the housing prices at a moderate level. For example, buyers of a second home are required to make a down payment of at least 50% of the value of the house, and banks are not allowed to lend to those who want to buy a third house. These are just two of the many regulations to keep the level of real estate speculation low. On the downside, this also drives a bigger sword between the rich and the poor in the country.

Taking the affordability of real estate into account many critics of the hukou system would end up being quiet, since this system at least prevents even worse prices and strong overpopulation in the major cities. In fact, those who criticise the hukou system oftentimes only see one side of the coin.

Thanks to numerous policies the housing prices in China are somewhat stable for the near future while the dilemma between improvable living standards and affordable housing prices still remains.

However, the government consistently tries to establish low-rent housing schemes in the major cities in China. In fact, it tried to improve the living conditions of many of the low-income urban households during the last decade, though it worked against market conditions that didn't make it easy for these measures to be as successful as one would like them to be.

While the government realizes the necessity for low-income housing in the cities, it also understands the importance of real-estate projects as a major driver of China's economic growth. Especially when combining the real estate business with the construction industry you can easily understand why it plays such an important role for China's GDP. This is not even taking into account all the other additional industries that benefit from this. Keep in mind, every new building needs lighting, electricity, etc.

In fact, the real-estate sector is one of the biggest beneficiaries of foreign direct investment (FDI) in China up until today. Thus, the early housing reform which originated under Deng's rule has not only improved the living condition in many parts of urban China, but also made the real-estate industry an important pillar for the overall economic growth with significant contributions to the GDP growth.

Despite the fact that real-estate is benefiting the most from FDI inflow into the country, housing supply in rural areas still largely depends on self-construction rather than subsidised housing projects, which further increases the disparity between rural areas and cities.

The Chinese government is trying to rebalance these developments and allow some people from rural areas free or strongly subsidised housing if they are willing to move to a new city, oftentimes in geopolitical and economical strategic area like west China. Some people decide to go and to give it a try, others prefer to stay where they are in the fear that they will lose their home and personal belongings for good without the chance to ever return.

Urbanization is also one of the major drivers of housing prices in China, as it is in almost all major cities all over the world. Especially in less developed regions and emerging economies we can observe how urbanization progression is faster than anywhere else in the world. To put this into perspective: Less developed regions are absorbing almost all of the population growth that is happening for the next ten years.

With more than 1.4 billion people it is not too surprising that China has the largest urban population in the world as it is also the most populous nation[36]. However, China has also a comparatively low urbanization level, one that is way lower than the global average. Thus, the overall proportion of the total population that is living in urban areas is not as high as in other countries, which is partly due to the urban restricting policies that stopped migration towards cities earlier in history – namely the previously introduced hukou system.

However, once Deng's reforms started, the urbanization level in China increased from only around 18 percent in the late 1970s to more than 40 percent in the early 2000s. It is even higher right now - around 58 percent - and it keeps increasing.

There are many benefits that come with the increasing urbanization in China and it is worth mentioning some. Education – a major objective and important aspect for the Chinese government – is easily accessible in cities and the overall level of this education is most of the times higher than in rural areas. In addition to that, benefits like better access to medical services and a higher level of social integration make urbanization important for China's future development and the overall welfare of its citizens. Despite all this, China is oftentimes faced with resource scarcity and is currently still accepting environmental degradation in order to achieve its objectives of high urbanization rates. Concrete, for example, a crucial component for construction work is said to be responsible for around 7% of the world's $CO_2$ emission. Half of the $CO_2$ emissions is created during the manufacturing of clinker, the most-energy intensive part of the cement-making process.

During a car drive from Beijing to the former Russian city of Dalian, I passed many cities that seemed to be more dead than alive. This was not a one-time experience and you will probably hear about it from many people who went outside the major cities. All across China you can find these "Ghost towns" that offer hundreds of high-rising apartments, parks, sculptures and even pre-built malls but are

---

[36] Just as a reference, the five biggest cities in China are: Chongqing with 30 million people, Shanghai with 26 million, Beijing with 22 million people, Chengdu with 16 million, and Tianjin with 15 million. As a comparison there are currently around 3.5 million people living in Berlin, 8 million in London, and 8.5 in New York.

inhabited by almost no people. These cities are all in fact still part of the urbanization plan of the Chinese government. In order to improve the living standard of people in rural parts of the country, the government decided to pre-build cities that could then be used by the rural population. What the government and many of the construction companies forgot was that once they offer the supply the demand has to follow in order to make it a successful venture. However, most people were and still are reluctant to give up their life on the farm as they fear that they are too old to move or that they will lose their houses once they leave the countryside. A one-way ticket into an uncertain future with no return. In addition to that, most of the people don't want to take the risk of moving to areas that are lacking basic public services like schools. As you can imagine this feeds into a vicious cycle as these would oftentimes only follow once enough people move to these new cities.

I am convinced, that at the end of the day many of these cities will be successful as the government wants to reach its target of moving more than 300 million people from rural areas into cities and there is not much space left in the old cities like Beijing and Shanghai. Thus, while some will succeed and be added to maps around the world others will fail as there is not enough pull to attract enough people. However, all of these failures don't matter too much to the government as long as the major objectives are reached and the overall living standards of most people are improved.

A great example of urbanization is the city of Chongqing. Chongqing itself has grown to an enormous size and makes cities like London and New York look like small suburbs. Chongqing city is the central point of a larger area designated as a municipality that hold a total population of more than 31 million. It is one of the largest cities on earth. However, this kind of urbanization is happening on a massive scale all over China and this trend is not expected to halt for the foreseeable future. Some expectations show that by 2050 around 1 billion to 1.1 billion people live in cities in China. However, even at that level, China may only be urbanized by around 70%. This compares with prevailing rates of around 90 percent for the United Kingdom and the United States, around 80 percent for France and Germany, and around 77 percent for Japan.

Together with the rapid urbanization rate and the many new cities that pop-up all over the country comes an alteration of the environment that currently seems unavoidable in order to achieve major objectives. For many years China was destroying huge parts of the natural habitat and emitting gigatons of greenhouse gasses into air. This in fact plays such an important role that we will look at environmental issues in a separate chapter. What we can conclude at this point already is that urbanization leads to destruction of natural landscape and increased greenhouse gas emissions. Supplementing this are additional indirect influences. For example, urbanization and the decrease in farm land indirectly influences food security in the country.

And while there are many ambitions from the government to drive a more environmentally focused approach, reality makes it a difficult venture. This, most likely is a development that needs to take place over many decades.

What we can take away from this chapter is that there are three main factors that are contributing to the "bubbly" housing market in China. One being the rapid urbanization that happened during the last decade. Second being the rising income inequality that followed Deng Xiaoping's opening up and third being the control of land ownership by local government.

In order to reduce the existing housing problem in China the Chinese government needs to focus its efforts and work on the three above mentioned factors. Only when income inequality is finally reduced to a healthier level and low-cost housing is more accessible for the poor, together with continuing regulation of housing speculation, can the Chinese housing market cool down again. If and how this happens is hard to tell. It is certain, though, that urbanization will play a central role for future policies and developments within China. In fact, further economic growth and social development will only continue to prioritize urbanization in the upcoming decades, making it important for us to have a general understanding and important for the Chinese government to follow clear objectives.

# TRANSPORTATION IN CHINA

# 运输

I n the last chapter we learned how China's appearance is
constantly changing with new cities emerging over just a few
years and existing cities constantly growing and improving over the
same course of time.

It is important to dedicate one chapter to transportation, though, as
it is equally important for China's economic growth and urbanization.
The Chinese government realized that in order to keep the economy
growing, they need a system that helps people to effectively move
goods from A to B and people across the country. A system that allows
for mobility, and decreases existing barriers.

An efficient, well-planned and modern transportation network
offers all this and probably more.

Going back in time, we can see that many European countries
promoted their transportation during the second world war as an
efficient way to quickly reach the factories and in order to push for
military success by being able to move men and weapons to the

frontiers in a fast way. During the years following the second world war many cities had to be rebuild and new transportation networks were created as a consequence as the opportunity was given to start from scratch.

Taking a step back and recalling what we learned from the first part of this book we can see that the China of the 19th and early 20th century, together with the western colonial powers built railroads connecting the historically important cities of China to each other and to the newly constructed treaty ports (the same ones that the colonial powers used to bring opium and other goods into the country). This system, together with some existing water ways allowed China to substantially grow once it used the existing network to export goods rather than to forcefully import opium.

In China, a country that reaches all the way from the middle east to the far east and from the cold north to the hot waters in the south, we can observe that transportation is one of the major components that is needed to boost economic growth in the county. Adding to urban transportation is the major so-called Belt and Road Initiative (BRI) with which China is trying to boost its economy for the upcoming years and to find new growth through construction projects abroad. However, China is also trying to increase the interdependence between itself and the many countries in Asia and the Middle east using the Belt and Road Initiative and the work of leading development banks. In the last chapter of this book we will have an in-depth look at the Belt and Road Initiative and learn about its role for the future of China.

In an era that is marked by climate change and an increasing number of calamities, the existing and newly emerging transportation systems in China must be able to weather all kinds of shocks. This does not stop at earthquakes, strong winds, or flooding but reaches as far as fuel shortages.

Therefore, the Chinese transportation systems need to cover a diverse range of choices in order to allow for a smooth commute and safe transportation. If the train isn't running due to disturbances then there need to be easily-accessible alternatives in place. In addition to that, we can observe how new technologies start to function as complementary goods to the already existing transportation methods in place. For example, bike sharing as a complement to the old-fashioned metro are maybe the most visible and famous example for China.

New forms of transportation are smoothly coexisting with the old systems, which allows citizens to increase the efficiency of their travel and shorten their daily commute while at the same time helps them to save valuable time for other things in life. In retrospect, it increases their comfort tenfold.

We do however also see substitutes emerging like solar powered buses that offer more than one benefit. They work as an alternative to the Metro, are not dependent on gasoline and offer an additional green alternative to classical busses or taxies. Seeing these benefits, it makes sense that the Chinese government is trying to increase the number of busses in use.

Additionally, many of the new transportation systems can be fuelled by multiple energy sources and are no longer dependent on one single source. Thus, if oil prices spike, the system can run on electricity that is only powered by the sun or the wind.

One characteristic of current infrastructure projects is that they are oftentimes taking into account the implications of climate change for China and they are trying to reduce the likelihood of being affected by future disasters that may threaten transportation infrastructure or important fuel sources. Access to enough fuel and gas resources for the future is also one major theme of the Belt and Road Initiative.

The Chinese government is formulating its strategic goals in so called five-year plans. In the most recent plan, it formulated some important goals that it wants to reach in the period 2015 to 2020. One goal in China's current five-year plan is aiming to increase the number of non-fuel driven vehicles in order to achieve a clear independence from oil supplying countries. The current aim of the government is to reach five million electric and hybrid cars driving on the roads in China by the year 2020. To achieve this, China bought 188,000 electric vehicles and plug-in hybrids in 2015 alone. For an economy with a population of around 1.3 - 1.4 billion this is just under one percent of the country's total car sales that year. But, while this might sound like an insignificant number, it still accounts for a 223 percent increase in sales compared to the previous year. With this growth, China's electronic vehicle market is growing faster than in any developed country around the world and is consequently becoming one of the most relevant and looked-after markets for manufacturers of electronic vehicles.

The bigger cities in China especially profit from the move to more electronic vehicles on the street. In Shenzhen the entire bus fleet is powered by solar power. In the Chinese capital, Beijing, the move to more electric vehicles went so far that the government required a minimum of 30 percent of municipal vehicles to be powered by battery or fuel cell by 2016. Right now, more than 100,000 electric buses (this makes around one-fifth of the nation's total number of busses) are on roads and the number is increasing every day. At the current rate, China's entire bus fleet could be completely electric by the year 2025, if not earlier.

In addition to that, Beijing and other cities offer preferential treatment to electric vehicles in their license plate lottery system and exempt these vehicles from alternate-day driving restrictions that became more and more common due to pollution. If you land in Shenzhen with a plane or arrive via the seaway you will easily notice that almost every taxi is nowadays powered by electricity rather than fuel. The usage of alternative fuels is not stopping on the busy streets of the city, tough.

Right now, most of the Chinese universities only allow electronic scooters and cars to enter the campus area, emphasising the strategic goals of the government to increase the number of electronic vehicles on the street and in use as substitutes to less environmentally friendly alternatives.

Since we already talked a bit about China's changing transportation landscape let's have a deeper look at other projects the Chinese government is currently undergoing in order to improve its public transportation. The first one to mention at this point and probably the other "major" transportation method next to the classic automotive is a so called "Bus Rapid Transit" (BRT) which I first encountered a few years ago in Jakarta, Indonesia. Later I came across the same system in China, though I have to admit that the Indonesian government adopted this from the Chinese and not the other way around. So, while China is the actual role model for the Indonesian BRT system, it still hasn't reached a point where it is planning to stop expanding its BRT systems. If we have a closer look at China, we can see that the bus rapid transit systems currently move over 4.5 million people every day from A to B[37].

In Guangzhou, the famous trading city in the Pearl River Delta, the bus rapid transit system includes elevated platforms for boarding and the system is furthermore efficiently integrated with the city's metro system and bike-sharing program making it an easy and convenient way of transportation for most of the population and a great alternative that helps to control the flow of people better.

Furthermore, China is now home to nearly 30 separately working metro systems in its major cities all across the country. Amongst these 30 metros we can even find four that are among the ten busiest systems in the world. Looking at the population size of most Chinese cities this is not too much of a surprise.

Due to the fact that China is trying to move more of its rural population into cities, new cities are emerging. In addition to that, smaller cities are growing into metropolitan areas due to economical improvements. Due to these reasons, seven more metros are currently under construction, and a total of 18 more are in the planning or early development stages. This trend will likely not reverse anytime soon.

Whoever had the chance to visit Beijing or Shanghai before will likely have noticed the enormous size of the metro systems and maybe

---

[37] Just as a comparison, in the United States this number is as low as 500.000 (Although it's worth mentioning that the U.S. population is only less than a quarter the size of the Chinese population).

even got lost in the huge stations. As a matter of fact, Shanghai's and Beijing's metro systems are spanning more than 500 km and are the longest and second-longest in the world, respectively.

Fun fact: Different to western countries where each metro system looks different for each city and has its own "style", the metro systems in China look almost identical from city to city.

China's many metro systems provide affordable mobility to its citizens, oftentimes just costing a few yuan, strengthening economic resilience. This is an important factor for further economic growth in the cities and oftentimes one of the multiple factors considered when moving to the city. Oftentimes transportation infrastructure is seen as a key component when promoting economic growth and development. The underlying logic is that you first need to have access to markets before you can actually profit from them. Improving the transportation infrastructure can create this access and additionally lead to an overall beneficial situation for the economy. The improved transportation infrastructure networks further increase the number of cities. These new cities help to create additional growth of already existing cities that function as engines of economic growth for the whole of China.

Adding to that is the fact that improved transportation infrastructure generally increases the access of rural regions to cities and the overall economy, letting them profit from the economic boom in regions like Chongqing and Guangzhou. These cities profit in return from available, low-cost labour that is willing to move from rural regions into the cities. This, despite the hukou system can be possible due to company sponsorship. Even if this is not given, people willingly leave their children and family behind to find working opportunities in the cities and the flourishing factories surrounded them. Those who remain in rural areas receive less and less economic and welfare benefits from the rapid urbanization as a result. Thus, widening the income gap between rural- and urban China even further.

We can conclude this part with a neutral outlook, taking into account that while China is genuinely profiting from the urban transportation networks, a good transportation infrastructure by itself does probably not do enough. What is needed is a functioning supply and demand that can be built on these networks, turning them into successful projects that bring prosperity.

Even though better transportation networks help to improve China's economy as a whole, factor mobility is still needed. Without factor mobility the increasing amount of investment might not be matched with a proper demand. In addition to that, it is important to keep a strategic focus that helps to assess return on investment on the projects that are undertaken.

# TECHNOLOGY IN CHINA

# 技术

While still being in the present we will talk about a topic that is probably closest to the future as it gets. In this chapter, we will talk about technology and technological advancement in China which would make for a great introduction into the third part of this book.

As in any country, China's technological development moved in stages with an initial slow start. We have seen how dynasties came and went, during which little seemed to be invented that would bring the country ahead. This was oftentimes followed by an apparently sudden flowering of creative talent.

The inventions during the $10^{th}$ until the $13^{th}$ century seem to be worth mentioning as several technologies still remain in use today. Just to mention a few: the windmill, mechanical clockwork, the lock gates that are used to control the flow of water in canals, power transmission through a drive belt, water-powered blowing engines, hemp-spinning machines, gear wheels, stern-post rudders for ships, water-powered trip hammers for forges, and so on. They all originated in China. Other inventions, such as gunpowder and printing, were also invented in China before they spread to the west, as mentioned earlier in this book.

Let's have a look at technology and its use in today's age. Everyone who's ever spent a few days in China in the last 10 years will have noticed that nothing (and I mean NOTHING!) works without a phone and stable internet connection. You order a taxi using your phone, pay at the grocery store, or buy insurance with just a few clicks. The government on the other hand is benefiting from this, too, and is getting better insight into the behaviours and activities of its citizens. This however, is not the only benefit for the government.

If you look closely, you can see how technology and interconnectivity have not only taken over everyday life but are also important for China's growth and success in a dynamic and globalized world.

The Chinese mindset of constant self-improvement oftentimes goes hand in hand with the rapid advancement in technology that we can observe in China. Chinese people, however, mostly care about two things though and those are increased convenience and climbing the social ladder. Over the years, the growth of the internet (the next chapter is solely dedicated to this) increased the level of convenience all over the world with a rapid speed.

Recent technological trends and the growth of applications like WeChat and MoBike are just two of many examples of how technology is allowing for more convenience in the everyday life of many Chinese. The author, Duncan Clark, found the perfect words to describe the new wave of technology in China: "Internet services in the west offer increasing convenience no doubt - but nothing beats the experience in China". If you are not yet convinced just try to buy an insurance in Europe and then try to do the same on WeChat – your experience will be very different.

In this chapter we will have a look at some examples to get a better feeling for the rise of technology and its use in China. For this, we will talk about some famous Chinese applications, technology companies, and have a look at how Robotics, AI and other concepts contribute to the overall success of China's technology sector.

Right now, nearly all of China's approximately 800 million internet users use smartphones to stay connected. At the same time, payments via QR codes, led by Tencent's WeChat and Alibaba's Alipay, are making cash an obsolete commodity of the past. If you look closely you can see how over the years following the internet boom WeChat has penetrated into the daily lives off almost all young Chinese and by now plays an important role in Chinese society. Mobile payments via scanned QR codes generated around 38 trillion RMB of volume in 2016, which is already over fifty times that of the US. Furthermore, the two leading providers of QR payments, Tencent and Alibaba, each have over 500m users on their platforms.

Currently, WeChat is the most widely used social media platform in the country and is unique in its characteristic that market, state and civil society all merge and compete on it. WeChat, in fact, is a phenomenon that many westerners find hard to understand and many are fascinated by once they do. In other emerging countries around the world it is met with curiosity and smartphone applications like the Indonesian "GoJek" try to learn from WeChat and duplicate some of its services to apply them to countries outside of China in the hopes of having similar success.

However, while China is now beginning to shape the future of the global tech landscape, so far nothing comes close to what WeChat is currently achieving in China. WeChat shows all of us tech-geeks what can be possible when an entire country uses one application.

WeiXin (微信) as WeChat is known in China means micro letter if you would translate it to English. In a way WeChat is similar to western communication platforms like Facebook's Messenger, WhatsApp, Instagram and Twitter[38]. You can use the app to talk to your friends, share photos and stay in contact with relatives who are living far away.

---

[38] With monthly active users (MAUs) of more than 550 million people WeChat is almost as big as Facebook's Messenger which has monthly active users of about 700 million people worldwide.

But WeChat goes beyond just staying in touch with old friends and family and offers additional functionality which makes it such a unique experience. In fact, the power of WeChat lies in its many layers of functionality.

WeChat can be used to pay for transaction in almost every store in China, online and offline for small things like a snack bar, bubble tea or bigger things like your new apartment and next vacation. In addition to that, China's WeChat can be used to hail a taxi, order food, buy movie tickets, insurance, flights, trains, pay bills, book doctor appointments, apply for visas, and so on. The list in fact is never-ending. It even has an official stamp of approval that in many situations replaces the government issued physical ID card for Chinese citizens. In addition to that, millions of applications live within WeChat which makes this Chinese messenger more similar to a browser than to a simple chatting application. Right now, there are more than 10 million so called "official accounts" that are owned by big corporations, small vendors, fashion brands, and celebrities. This list, too, can go on and on. These official accounts include exclusive application programming interfaces (so called APIs) that allow for a unique user experience that differs for each vendor. The unique APIs of many accounts allow for an app-within-an-app experience that makes WeChat so powerful. Similar (yet still different) to the American Apple Pay, WeChat brings many of these applications together in its payment system which serves as a cornerstone of the application.

WeChat's "Wallet" allows one to link their bank account to the application and thus moves the bank account away from the classic credit card to an all-electronic, always available service. WeChat Wallet transforms the classical bank account into a modern, frictionless transaction tool that allows for instant payment.

Chinese consumers live their lives in symbiosis with their mobile devices and running out of battery is close to a catastrophic event. It cuts you off from conversations, payments and makes it hard to get back home from your recent trip to the shopping mall.

There is another aspect to WeChat and that is the political aspect. Tencent, like many tech companies, is complying with the strict Chinese information controls and dependent on the goodwill of the Communist Party. As a consequence, WeChat is enforcing censorship and surveillance where necessary that allows to narrow the access to news and information. The strong government-driven censorship makes it hard for Chinese citizens to get an objective view on political issues taking place inside and outside their country. In many instances there are no reports at all on political charged developments. In the very beginning there weren't even reports on the 2019 protest in Hong Kong. If you report and raise your voice on platforms on WeChat, you expose yourself to the supervision of the government and will be in fear of some consequences.

Using WeChat means giving the company, and the government access to conversations, transaction data, and location 24/7. Users can be monitored in almost everything they do. Additionally, enforcing penalties is made easier due to the fact that real-name registration is necessary in order to use WeChat and its features[39]. Keep in mind, all the information that Tencent is collecting is available to the police if necessary.

Let's move on and look at another example of the technological advancement in China - The rise of dock-less bikes across the country. These bikes line-up and pile-up in the streets of China's cities and fill the exits of almost every major Metro station across the country.

They say a decade in China only lasts for five years and if you would have visited Beijing a few years ago you wouldn't have found a single dock-less bike in the city. Now, it is hard to find a part of any major city that is free of dock-less bikes. It seems like new social conventions and massive technology companies can pop-up seemingly overnight in China.

---

[39] Once you start using WeChat everything is linked together. Your phone is linked with WeChat, WeChat is linked with your bank account, you are linked with your friends, and they in return are linked to their bank accounts, phone numbers, and so on.

The leading bike-sharing firms, MoBike and Ofo, were founded in 2015 and 2014, respectively. Ofo in fact was founded by students at my alma mater Peking University but in the end proved to be less competitive against the strong venture capital backed MoBike which is dominating more and more inside and outside of China. The market for dock-less bikes went from 0 to 100 in just a few years. However, despite their innovative product, many bike-sharing companies break under the fierce competition in the market.

Companies thus get creative and MoBike, the biggest bike-sharing company by far in China, is profiting from a deposit approach in which users have to deposit a required amount in order to use the service. These deposits allow for a safety pillow that can be used when needed. The initial deposit for MoBike is around 299 RMB[40]. In addition to that, MoBike is generating around 0.5 RMB per half an hour use. Using a so called MoBike pass customers can sign up for monthly, quarterly, half-year or yearly memberships. Besides that, MoBike is profiting from a relatively long average useful life of around four years per bike that can be achieved without much maintenance. In 2017 the number of MoBike users was around 20 million. This would make around 2 billion in yearly income if every user would subscribe for two half-year plans per calendar year[41].

There is another company that is disrupting the transportation market, though in a very different way. Didi Chuxing (滴滴出行), a Chinese ride-hailing company is oftentimes referred to as the Chinese version of Uber. In a way it is, but a bit more complex and closer to cutting-edge technology than its American counterpart, I would say. If you read up on Didi[42], as it is mainly known in mainland China, you will find it categorised as an app-based transportation service that is not limited to car hailing like Uber but also includes taxi hailing, on

---

[40] Pricing strategies (especially for Chinese companies) can change fast, so this number might be out of date by the time you read this.

[41] The actual valuation is of course a bit more sophisticated than this. However, it should still give you a general idea about the revenue that MoBike is able to generate.

[42] Didi or 弟弟 means younger brother when translated into English which I always found entertaining. The company itself is written 滴滴 unfortunately.

demand delivery services, automobile services and even co-development of vehicles with other leading Chinese companies.

Currently, Didi is the absolute dominating power in the ride-hailing business in China. In a remarkable Harvard Business School case study beautify written by Alice M. Tybout you can read about Uber entering the Chinese market and I can only recommend you to read it. In this book, I will not go into too much detail as I would not be able to explain it any better than the case study did. I can and will however spoil it for you and tell you that it ended with Didi acquiring Uber in 2016. With this deal, Uber gained around 5.9% stake in the combined company and preferred equity interest that is equal to about 17.7%.

Didi Chuxing's operation is huge. To get a better understanding for how huge it actually is, we should have a closer look at Didi's operations: The Taxi servicing is operated by around 2 million drivers in over 400 cities in China and Brazil. In addition to that, the Express service, the counterpart to the classic uber e-hailing, provides around 2.4 million rides every day. Furthermore, Didi is also rapidly expanding beyond China's first- and second-tier cities into the more underdeveloped regions of the country. For example, right now Didi's service covers 518 out of China's 823 underdeveloped regions[43].

Probably the most interesting (and maybe less talked about) part about Didi Chuxing is its smart transportation brain. This is Didi's cutting-edge AI and cloud technology segment that is focused on developing smart traffic lights and optimized traffic management systems.

Another company that is redefining what AI and big data analytics can do is the Chinese company Baidu. Baidu is a technology company that is focused on internet related services, similar to Alphabet in the United States. Thus, it is not too surprising that Baidu is offering a Chinese search engine, as well as a mapping service, similar to Google Maps, called Baidu Maps. Baidu's expertise is in its Research with a strong focus on machine learning and AI. Until 2017 the chief scientist at Baidu Research was no one less than Andrew Ng.

---

[43] Again, let me warn you as these numbers might have already changed.

Some of the best works and breakthroughs of Baidu are in the field of natural language processing. This includes applying machine learning concepts to speech recognition and voice synthesis. When applying machine learning packages to speech concepts, the algorithm is searching through huge databases of known language data to better understand patterns and leverage those. This is known as deep learning. Thankfully, Baidu is profiting from a huge number of available datasets due to the low concern towards privacy issues in China. Thanks to this, Baidu is able to train thousands of labelled audio data to its so-called neural network. As a consequence, this neural network learns to associate different sounds with certain words or phrases which can be leveraged in a number of ways.

Let's look at another topic. China has over 100 cities with populations of at least one million. This compares Europe with only around 34 cities. Zhengzhou, a tier two city in Henan province, that you probably never heard of before has a bigger population than the whole of Denmark. This consequently leads to China having more millennials than the US has people and more internet users than almost any other country in the world.

As a consequence of this and the underdeveloped retail channel in many second and third tier cities, ecommerce in China is an important driver of new business - totalling more than 42% of the world's online retail transactions. This fast shift to ecommerce has been extremely disruptive to the traditional retail model and made it almost impossible for traditional brick-and-mortar businesses to survive nowadays without a functioning ecommerce integration.

Analogous to the western FANGs, Baidu, Alibaba, Tencent and JD.com, are also better known as BATJs by foreigners and oftentimes referenced to as the Google, eBay, Facebook and Amazon of the country.

Alibaba has about 70% share of the Chinese ecommerce market via its two platforms, Taobao and Tmall. Tencent on the other hand has a billion strong monthly active user base through WeChat. They are thus not only the biggest, but also the most influential players in the country. JD.com, the third player in this area, is China's biggest retailer, expanding from its dominating position in electronics and appliances into other markets making it an almost perfect counterpart to Amazon. Baidu is known as the Google of China with a dominant and market leading share of searches - even higher than Google's share in the US market (Yes, that is possible).

Having a closer look at the above-mentioned player, we can see that Alibaba owns Youku (a streaming website similar to YouTube), Baidu owns iQiyi (a video platform similar to Netflix) and Tencent follows a similar business model to Disney. Additionally, Tencent also holds the title as the biggest computer game company in the world - an industry that is three times bigger than global box office receipts. Tencent earns nearly half of its revenues from hosting and developing online games!

As you hopefully can see by now, China is no longer the huge warehouse that some foreigners still think China is.

As a matter of fact, most parts of China can no longer be seen as low-income and emerging, but rather as developed and cutting-edge. They already emerged and China is now leading in many fields from speech recognition to robotics. During my time in Shenzhen I had more exposure to modern edge-cutting technology than ever before in my life. It is a global hot spot for innovation and pragmatism, two main drivers that were responsible for China's success in the world of AI and robotics. Soon, an entrepreneur-driven China will reshape some facets of our future and introduce more innovations that will in turn find copycats all around the world. With growing strength in fields ranging from artificial intelligence and batteries all the way to genomics, China is already one of the most innovative places I have seen in my life and will soon be one of the major drivers of change in the world.

Already today, China has the largest number of unicorns outside the US. In addition to that, it overtook Europe as a prime destination for venture capital in 2014, according to research by the accounting firm PricewaterhouseCoopers. Currently, three of the world's top five most highly valued private companies are Chinese. One being the previously introduced ride-hailing goliath Didi Chuxing, one being the phone (and everything else) maker Xiaomi, and one being the e-commerce firm Meituan-Dianping.

From our Baidu example we can learn about an additional reason for China's success. While many western companies struggle to utilize the data they collect in order to improve their service, Chinese companies already have an easy access to vast reams of data, generated by the hundred millions of users. In addition to that, the centralized structure that finds its origin in the communist system of the country, simplifies the access to the millions of data that can be used to optimize and leverage existing business models.

One question that always gets asked in these situations of rapid growth is how it is possible to sustain it over time. Currently, the intense competition between the country's internet giants is one reason for the growth as all of them try to increase their market share by having competitive prices. Another factor that is contributing to a sustained growth is the willingness of Chinese consumers to stay open-minded and to embrace new developments and change.

We can see how the tech-fight between the US and China slowly intensifies more and more. A recent example of this, following the initial trade tensions between the two, is China's so called 3-5-2 initiative. This new directive aims to decrease the exposure to foreign computer equipment and software within the next three years within China and consequently boost the local, home-grown technology industry. The rate of change is fast as you will see when you look closer at the meaning of 3-5-2. The Chinese government wants to reduce the reliance on foreign (and surprisingly predominantly American) technology at a rate of 30% in 2020, 50% in 2021 and the remaining 20% in 2022. This development is taking place under the Chinese Cyber Security Law, which aims to benefit homegrown companies such as Lenovo, Huawei, and Xiaomi, just to mention a few.

Looking closer, it becomes imminent to think that this is a drastic move as China is one of the biggest import markets of PCs and PC equipment manufacturers in the world and an important driver of growth in this area.

While 3-5-2 improves the outlook for Chinese brands, obstacles remain in place that will likely make it difficult for China to fully rely on its domestic supply chain within the next few years. One major obstacle is on the software-side rather on the hardware-side. Many systems either run on macOS or Windows and being able to use these systems is a basic foundation to have. Using a homegrown alternative to the two leading operating systems makes it difficult to find foreign software used in automation, construction and other industrial areas. Poor user experience, missing compatibility and skill are making software a very difficult issue for China to overcome. With increasing tension between China and the US we can expect this trend to continue and we might see a reliable alternative to MacOS and Microsoft Windows soon.

What we can take away in the end is that convenience is the new religion in China. Innovation its gospel. There are many more examples of China's technology and its development cited in literature.

Despite China's innovative power, the strong scale advantages that comes with 1.4 billion Chinese people living in the Mainland is crucially important for the success of many unicorns and technology companies. Sure, a good business idea is important, good execution and investors that help with the venture funding are oftentimes necessary. However, the main driver of success comes from being able to provide service at low costs and the millions of customers that can make even a bad business profitable.

Something that we should not forget is that China will have a major impact on future technological improvements and trends due to these advantages that allow many companies to grow and prosper. The wealth of data and information will lead a new revolution of Internet of things (IoT), deep learning, and constant innovation.

# INTERNET IN CHINA

# 互联网

Electronic computers existed since the 1950s and around fifteen years later the history of the internet officially began when Robert Tayler and Lawrence Roberts worked on an package-switching network called ARPANET. In its early days the "Internet" was still very primitive yet we can say in retrospect ground-breaking and world changing.

The first ever use of the ARPANET was described by Gregory Gromov as follows: "We set up a telephone connection between us and the guys at SRI. We typed the L and we asked on the phone, 'Do you see the L?'; 'Yes, we see the L,' came the response. We typed the O, and we asked, 'Do you see the O?'; 'Yes, we see the O.' Then we typed the G, and the system crashed".

From there the development did not stop and twenty-five years later the first website went live. As of 2018 around 4 billion people are using the internet for a variety of things. I can assure you, having access to the internet made it a lot easier to write this book.

From the 4 billion users around 802 million are living in China[44]. This makes around 58 percent of the population of the country and makes it by far the biggest internet user base in the world by total number.

The Internet in China arrived as soon as 1994, soon after Deng Xiaoping opened up China to the rest of the world. Only a few years afterwards (around 1997) did the Ministry of Public Security take its first steps to control the Internet, when it issued multiple comprehensive regulations governing the use of it. As Deng Xiaoping used to say: "If you open the window, both fresh air and flies will be blown in" (打开窗户，新鲜空气和苍蝇就会一起进来).

The Chinese government is aware of this and sees the Internet "inside" the country as part of the country's sovereignty. As a consequence, it should also be governed by the country itself.

Out of this early and growing regulation grew the famous "Great Firewall of China" which is a combination of legislative decisions and their subsequent technological enforcement. The list of blocked websites in China is long and would probably fill more than a page, maybe even more than this chapter. To give a general overview I do want to mention a few well-known websites and/or applications that are currently blocked in China: Instagram, Twitter, WhatsApp, Snapchat, Pinterest, Soundcloud, Facebook, Google, YouTube, Vimeo, Netflix, Amazon Prime Video, Hulu, Twitch, Spotify, Dropbox, The New York Times, The Wall Street Journal, The Economist, Bloomberg, Reuters… This list could go on and on.

As a consequence, the Great Firewall of China allowed many local technology companies to prosper in China. As we have seen in the previous chapter, companies like Baidu provide similar services like their American counterpart but profit from the fact that there is no natural competition from other market leaders outside of China. A perfect environment to grow tech start-ups to full grown unicorns.

---

[44] According to Chinese government data.

It probably comes to no one's surprise that with an increasing importance of Internet in China, Cyber-security became an issue of growing importance to the country, too. Personal information is available in abundance ranging from e-commerce and gaming to education and banking. With the enormous amount of data that is now available online a vast range of organisations and governments become an increasingly attractive target of cyber-attacks. These are attempts to expose, disable, steal, or to gain unauthorized access.

The 20th of September 1987 is a special day as it marks the day of the first ever email in China. It says "Across the Great Wall we can reach every corner in the world". It is quite funny to read this email more than thirty years later.

Fast forward from September 1987 China grew the world's most active social media environment with more than 700 million active users today. These 700 million users also spend more than 40% of their time online which makes them an important market for many businesses and a crucial channel for e-commerce marketing.

Over the years following the tremendous growth of many social-networking sites, a new challenge came in the way of the government's censorship ambitions – China's citizen now have easy access to various foreign information which oftentimes oppose the government's views. In addition to that, "influencers" play an increasingly important role in building opinions and consumer behaviour. For example, research indicates that around two-thirds of the Chinese rely on recommendations from friends and family while only one-third of US citizens does the same. This again is causing a big change – not only in the government's approach – but also in how marketing and advertising is changing over the coming years.

Adding to this is the fragmented structure of the social-media landscape which is adding another layer of complexity to the equation.

All of these factors are making the "Great Firewall of China" an increasingly complex structure that is getting harder and harder to control, while it consumes resources at a fast and growing rate.

While the internet brought new opportunities to many of the citizens of China and the country as a whole, it also brought additional challenges for local- and national authorities. China's Internet is like a Blackbox in which things work differently than outside. This allowed and allows for some different and unique developments and innovations that might have not existed otherwise.

# FINANCIAL MARKETS IN CHINA

# 金融市场

China's financial markets have been developing with a rapid pace since the late 1980s. Aligned with Deng Xiaoping's market reforms and the liberalization of the Chinese economy, the financial markets in China started to develop with a rapid pace. Over the years the Chinese financial markets developed into sizable markets thanks to enhanced market infrastructures, a better legal system and improved regulation.

In China, a variety of financial products are available in the market. Looking at equity markets we have A shares, which are common shares denominated in RMB and B shares, which are domestically listed shares traded in US dollar or HK dollars. Furthermore, there are securities investment funds, treasury bonds, corporate bonds, convertible bonds, commodity futures, ETF, LOF, warrants, and many more niche products.

Let's first take a more detailed look at equity markets. A shares are common shares that are issued by incorporated companies. These companies have to be registered in Mainland China and the shares have to be traded by domestic entities or retail investor [45] in Chinese currency. If a company wants to offer A shares it has to first submit an application to the CSRC, the China Securities Regulatory Commission, and meet the requirements laid out in relevant laws and regulations.

B shares on the other hand are denominated in the local currency, renminbi, but are offered and traded in foreign currencies. The inception of B shares is an important milestone for the country as it marks the first step in an internationalization of China's financial markets.

Additionally, China has four commodity futures [46], more than hundreds of futures brokerage firms, and a multitude of commodity transactions, including agricultural products such as beans, wheat, and cotton and industrial products such as copper, aluminium, and oil.

Over the past two decades a main focus was the development of new financial products in the Mainland. To understand financial markets in China, it is important to understand how crucial the first decade of the 21$^{st}$ century has been for China. It marks a period of crucial developments of China's securities market. In recent years, the Chinese securities market has been undergoing even further adjustments and transformation, closing the gap between foreign and Chinese markets. Non-tradeable shares, as a component of financial markets, have been important for the development of the equity market, in particular. These non-tradable shares have driven big equity market movements since the early 2000s.

To understand financial markets in China one date is of utmost importance to its development. In December of 2001 China entered into the World Trade Organization (WTO) and with it, it committed on specific guidelines regarding the securities sector. To name just the

---

[45] Excluding investors from Taiwan, Hong Kong, and Macau.
[46] Zhengzhou Commodity Exchange (ZCE, established in 1993), Dalian Commodity Exchange (DCE, established in February, 1993), Shanghai Futures Exchange (SHFE, established in 1999), and China Financial Futures Exchange (CFFEX, established in Shanghai in September, 2006).

most important ones: Foreign securities firms are allowed to engage directly in B share business (without Chinese intermediaries), representative offices in China of foreign securities firms may become Special Members of Chinese stock exchanges and an IPO of a company should meet a number of requirements ( e.g. have a complete and well-functioning organizational structure, be capable of making profits continuously in sound financial conditions, have no record of false financial statements for the previous 3 years and no record of other wrongdoings).

Let's look at another important market – the bond market. The size of the worldwide bond market is estimated at USD100 trillion. The bond market is part of the credit market, which in return is three times the size of the worldwide equity market. China has a multitier trading market for bonds. This does not only include the exchange bond market, but also the so called interbank bond market, and the over-the-counter (OTC) market.

Another important date to learn about is July 1981, which happened to be the date the first treasury bonds (T-bonds) was issued in China, following the communist rule over the country. Only six years later, a secondary market for T-bonds was established in Mainland China.

The first two stock exchanges were located in Shanghai and Shenzhen, respectively. Shortly thereafter, local governments set up additional 29 securities exchanges and more than 40 OTC markets across the country.

At present there are two major stock exchanges in China - the Shanghai and Shenzhen stock exchange. Both of them under the strict supervision of the China Securities Regulatory Commission (CSRC).

The Shanghai stock exchange was founded on the 26th of November 1990, the Shenzhen stock exchange was established shortly thereafter on the first December 1990. The Shanghai stock exchange is the world's 4th largest stock market by market capitalization at USD4 trillion [47]. The Shenzhen stock exchange recorded a market

---

[47] As of November 2018.

capitalization of USD2.5 trillion in 2018, which makes it the 8th largest stock exchange in the world[48].

Similar to other parts of China's financial markets the money market is strongly impacted and characterised by the reforms that followed Deng Xiaoping's opening-up policy. There are four submarkets that combined make the Chinese money market. These are the renminbi (RMB) lending market, the repo market[49], the bond market, and the bills market. Part of the strong impact of the money market was the development of the Central Bank's monetary policy. The People's Bank of China is the authority in charge of the Chinese money market and was formed in 1948 out of the merger of Huabei Bank, Beihai Bank, and Xibei Farmer Bank. It wasn't until 1983, though, that the State Council made the People's Bank of China (PBC) the official Central Bank of the country.

Deng Xiaoping is supposed to have said that "banks should be changed intro real banks", because he believed that under Mao's communist regime they have been nothing more than "money printing enterprises, cash vaults, but not real banks".

For the early days the Chinese banking system was organised around the People's Bank of China. However, executing on Deng Xiaoping's plans the PBC was turned into a supervisory body and central bank, while commercial activities and treasury functions were transferred to other entities. This happened around March 2003 when the State Council separated the supervisory responsibilities of the People's Bank of China over banking institutions, asset management companies, trust, and investment companies, and other depository financial institutions. This was also when the China Banking Regulatory Commission

---

[48] As a reference point, the biggest Stock exchange in the world is the New York stock exchange (NYSE) with an market capitalization of around USD22.9 trillion. The London Stock Exchange (LSE) has a market capitalization of around USD3.8 trillion, listing on number seven. On number three is the biggest stock exchange in Asia, the Japan stock exchange (JPX) with a market capitalization of around USD5.7 trillion – as of November 2018.

[49] The repurchase "repo" market, is a marketplace where banks lend cash to other institutions in exchange for collateral like government debt.

(CBRC) was established as a consequence to supervise the financial industry.

While we now have a basic understanding of the different parts of the financial markets in China you might not be aware of the enormous size of China's banking sector. It had an estimated size of total assets of USD40.1 trillion in the first quarter of 2019. This makes it the largest banking sector in the world by assets, even bigger than the US banking sector.

Also important to know is the concept of the "big four" (四大国有商业银行) which are the four biggest state-owned commercial banks in the country. These are the Bank of China, the China Construction Bank, the Industrial and Commercial Bank of China, and the Agricultural Bank of China, all of which are among the largest banks in the world as of 2018. Equally important but less famous are China Merchants Bank and the Shenzhen based Ping An Bank.

Bank of China, handles all dealings in foreign exchange and is responsible for allocating the country's foreign exchange reserves and carrying out all financial transactions with foreign firms. The Agricultural Bank on the other hand aims to facilitate financial operations in the rural areas. It issues loans and carries out overall supervision of rural financial affairs. The China Construction Bank managed state appropriations and loans for capital construction. Thus, it ensures that the funds were used for their designated purposes. Industrial and Commercial Bank of China (ICBC) is the largest bank in the world by total assets.

There are three "policy" banks to know about, the Agricultural Development Bank of China (ADBC), China Development Bank (CDB)[50], and the Export-Import Bank of China (Chexim or EXIM). These banks are responsible for financing economic and trade development as well as state-invested projects.

---

[50] Famous large-scale infrastructure projects include the Three Gorges Dam and the Shanghai Pudong International Airport. The bank is oftentimes described as the engine that powers the government's economic development policies.

Western nations like the US have accused China of using its government-controlled banking industry to further China's military goals partly through the Belt and Road Initiative and partly through the Maritime Silk Road.

Throughout the history of the People's Republic of China the government has exercised close control over financial transactions and the money supply.

We have seen however how between the 1990s and 2000s, China's banking system underwent significant changes, following Deng Xiaoping's opening-up policy. Chinese banks are now functioning more like Western banks and the system is overall more open and dynamic than it used to be. Nevertheless, China's banking industry still remains in the government's hands. The financial markets and the banking system in particular are a great example for a capitalist system under communist rule or a "Socialist system with Chinese characteristics". Furthermore, the Chinese banking system has been transformed from a formerly mono-banking system (with a single bank) into a system with a congregation of banking institutions. As many other things in China, the banks are oftentimes huge and so are the issues they carry with them.

Corruption, a very different topic, used to be and still partly is characteristic for the financial system. It should also be mentioned that state banks commonly receive huge government bailouts. Infrastructure projects are sometimes still allocated in a nepotist way and in some instances the pensions of hundreds of millions of elderlies have simply gone missing over the years.

# PAYMENT SYSTEMS IN CHINA

# 支付系统

After talking about technology, internet, and financial markets in China, let's have a quick look at payment systems before moving on to another topic.

The 16th Federal Reserve Chairman Jerome Powell once said in one of his speeches: "An efficient payments system provides the infrastructure needed to transfer money in low-cost and convenient ways. Efficient systems are innovative in improving the quality of services in response to changing technology and changing demand."

China's payment system is built on digital wallets rather than real ones and centres around the two big tech firms Alibaba and Tencent. Alipay is offered by Alibaba and WeChat Pay by Tencent.

China's payment system is changing the landscape of banking in China and is taking away an important source of bank revenues. Consequently, an alternative payment ecosystem is at work that interacts between merchants, consumers, and payment system providers.

With this new system there are new incentives that could realign existing business models and relationships between merchants, banks, and technology providers.

Tencent's WeChat Pay first rolled out around Lunar New Year 2014 offering so called "Red Envelopes[51]" that could be gifted to other people. WeChat offered a digital alternative to real envelopes, which together with the social media aspect of the application turned out to be a huge success and offered a lot of synergies. In 2014, the year WeChat Pay launched, around 16 million packages were sent. Just one year later this number grew to 1 billion. 2016 and 2017 the numbers grew even further to 8 billion and 46 billion, respectively. China's new payment system exploded in just a few years.

By now over 90 percent of people in China's Tier 1 cities use WeChat and Alipay as their primary payment method, with cash second, and card-based transaction as a third alternative that is barely touched.

One of the key benefits of mobile payment services such as WeChat is that they have alternative sources of data on which they can base crucial financial decisions such as providing credit. In China, software companies such as Tencent have access to a broader set of information regarding a customers' financial life, that a classic banking institute would not have. Just as an example, a commercial bank's knowledge over its customer is limited to data provided by that person and the bank probably does not know the exact relationship of everyone who sends money to the clients account but knows only the amount and the name of the sender. In contrast, merging the social media network of WeChat with the digital payments allows to draw a clearer picture. For example, WeChat is able to see into your network both socially and financially and knows about the different relationships in the

---

[51] It is common in China to give cash during Chinese new year, particularly between family members. This oftentimes happens in form of red envelopes. These red envelopes (also known as Hóngbāo) are also given during other special occasions such as weddings, graduation or the birth of a baby. The red colour of the envelope symbolizes good luck in Asian culture.

network and can even analyse patterns in payments using big data analytics.

A lot of incentives exist that encourage moving the payment system from banking to technology firms. There is a potential for anti-competitive behaviour and also privacy concerns as the vast amount of data collected makes the customer almost completely transparent. One problem is that it is not clear whether these concerns can be alleviated by more regulation. However, combining the vast amount of information at hand regarding social connectivity and financial flows between people and businesses opens up a new possibilities and might change the way lending works in the future.

Mobile payments in China have reached over USD40 trillion annually and the market is dominated by the two big players Alipay and WeChat Pay. Alipay holds around 53% market share and WeChat Pay around 39%. Today, both platforms have over a billion users on each of their platforms. By now China's digital payment system has more or less replaced cards and cash and changed the way companies interact with their customers. Even homeless people now ask for money using QR codes rather than their old metal cups or hats.

We can most certainly assume that China is likely to keep this alternative payment system and build on it rather than replace it. Additionally, foreign businesses serving Chinese retail customers will likely have to adopt further to Chinese payment platforms. When travelling to prominent holiday destinations for Chinese tourist you can observe how their payment system is already following them abroad. Thus, it is likely to assume that while China's payment system is likely to stay it is also likely to be further integrated into global payment systems.

We can conclude that China's payment system has grown into a system that is based on the combination of non-bank payment platforms and QR codes. This stands in sharp contrast to the well-established western bank card-based model led by companies like Visa or American Express. China's new payment system is here to stay.

Rather than disappearing it will continue to grow domestically and globally, following Chinese travellers and consumers abroad.

# SUSTAINABILITY IN CHINA

# 可持续发展

After learning about many aspects of present day China and spending quite some time on technological advancements that happened in the country it is now time to look at a very different topic. The topic of this chapter is sustainability and environmental change in China. For this we will not only talk about sustainability and environmental protection but also look at recycling in China.

China's environmental policy is oftentimes compared to that of the United States prior to 1970, because while there are relatively strict regulations, the actual monitoring and enforcement of these regulations is in some areas flawed. Oftentimes monitoring is undertaken by local governments and they are not only more exposed to corruption but also interested in economic growth rather than sustainable development and environmental protection. In addition, non-governmental work from NGOs can sometimes be restricted by the communist and centralised government.

That being said, the Chinese communist party understands the risk of environmental damage and has a strong focus on decreasing pollution and moving to a more sustainable approach. For example, fighting increasing pollution is a major task for the government as they see it as a necessary development in building a well-off society. To achieve this, the old-fashioned and oftentimes inefficient approach of traditional focus on purely economic growth with high pollution, high consumption, and extremely negative environmental effects, is not sustainable anymore.

It is increasingly important that these new ambitions are driven by the government on the one hand, and financial players on the other. For many people, especially in emerging markets, environmental concern is oftentimes only present if it directly impacts their lives. While many people in Beijing are concerned about the pollution people in smaller coastal cities may have other concerns. If you visit Beijing – especially during the winter month – you will easily have one or two days where the city is covered in smog. Wearing air pollution mask already became a daily routine for China's 1.4 billion citizen and while the situation in cities like Beijing and Shanghai is improving it is only getting worse in many other cities in north China.

In the west we oftentimes talk about environmental, social, and governance factors to look at a country's sustainable development. These three factors are bundled under the simple abbreviation "ESG." Looking at western countries these ESG efforts oftentimes follow a bottom-up level with the company being a major driver in the integration effort. In contrast to that, ESG integration efforts in China are oftentimes driven from a top-down approach, with the government being a major force that drives ESG integration from a social and regulatory standpoint. Thus, it is not surprising that the central government continuously emphasizes ecological and environmental protection and focuses on sustainable development.

The China Society for Finance and Banking published a paper in December 2018 in which they lay out the "Green Investment Principles for the Belt and Road" with the goal to incorporate low-carbon and sustainable development into the Belt and Road Initiative. We will talk about this initiative in the third part of this book.

If we break down the different aspects of environmental issues into pollution, water, forest and general ESG aspects, we can see that while environmental issues have increased in correlation with China's opening-up to the western world, Xi Jinping's China is more committed to fight these issues.

Since Deng Xiaoping's early days various forms of pollution have increased in China as the country increasingly industrialized and grew to be the factory of the western world. This however has caused widespread environmental and health issues across Mainland China. As a natural reaction, the government responded with increasing environmental regulations and innovation to fight the increasing pollution.

Fighting environmental issues is not only important from a social and environmental standpoint but also from a political one. If China wants to become a first world country and leader in in the Asian hemisphere it has to show the world that it can overcome environmental challenges. Beijing, China's current capital, together with Shanghai is the figurehead of China's development.

The number of domestic and international tourists visiting Beijing totalled 285 million in 2016 alone and both of these cities are the most visible for foreign eyes. However, Beijing, which lies in a topographical bowl and heats with coal, is subject to heavy air pollution during the winter months. According to a report published by Greenpeace and Peking University's School of Public Health in December 2012, the coal industry is responsible for the highest levels of air pollution with around 19 percent, followed by vehicle emissions which contributes to approximately 6 percent. The issues arises because coal is still used as the primary fuel to power China's gigantic and growing industrial sector. In January 2013, fine airborne particulates that pose the largest health risks, rose as high as 993 micrograms per cubic meter in Beijing. And while the number is decreasing, China's pollution levels are still far from the World Health Organization's (WHO) guideline of no more than 25 microgram per cubic meter. Another big contributor next to the coal industry is car ownership. On the World Bank's list of the twenty most polluted cities on earth, sixteen are located in China. In 2018, China added a record 23 million new cars to the already existing fleet and car ownership reached 240 million. This number is increasing by tens of millions every year and China's need and rush to develop electric vehicles becomes more and more obvious.

Looking at another environmental issue impacting China, water resources, we can see similar trends to air pollution. China's water resources are affected by both severe water quantity shortages and severe water quality pollution. When looking at the rapid economic growth and the increasing population size that happened over the last few decades it becomes easy to see how water demand and pollution are impacted. China did not stand around and wait though but instead focused on building water infrastructure, as well as increasing regulation around this topic. The need for technological advancement becomes clear when considering that the many coal-fired power stations in northern China not only pollute the air but also demand high usage of water. Consequently, these coal-fired power stations are drying-up northern China.

This problem is partly imported, showing the flipside of the fast economic growth of the country. The many factories that have been set up all across China by multinational companies have not only turned China into the factory of the capitalist world but also turned the country into the garbage yard of the world. Consequently, by January 2018 China announced its so called "National Sword Policy" in which the country banned the importation of certain types of solid waste and set strict contamination limits on recyclable materials.

Forests in China are exposed to similar threats and impacted by the vast amount of waste, fast industrialisation, and the lack of commitment to sustainability. China's forest cover around 21% of the country - considering the size of the country this is quite a big number.

The United Nations Environment Programme (UNEP) repeatedly lists China amongst the top 15 countries with the highest amount of old-growth forest[52]. From the 21 percent around half are old-growth forest, which sums to more than 111 million hectares[53]. More than one-third of these old-growth forest are under immense pressure from the high population densities and the related consequences.

Over the last 50 years China has turned into the fastest-growing market for timber products and paper pulp in the world. The impact of this is disastrous for the world's primary forest and for China's sustainable future. The consequences reach way outside Mainland China, though. The once untouched rainforests in Indonesia, Myanmar, and central Africa - places known as the "lungs of the planet" for their work in turning carbon dioxide into breathable oxygen - are disappearing at unprecedented rates to satisfy the never-ending Chinese demand for more. Just to put this into perspective, in Indonesia, home to Orangutans and Komodo dragons, an area the size of Switzerland gets illegally logged each year. Emphasis here is on illegally, as the area that allocated for legal logging is even bigger. Although reserves of famous hardwoods like teak or meranti are virtually exhausted illegal logging syndicates found a new source of income, selling protected merbau trees, logged in remote provinces such as Papua. Oftentimes, Malaysian or Indonesian logging companies use falsified documents and globally connected warehouses in Singapore to sell their products. Their middlemen are oftentimes based in Hong Kong, who make sure that the illegal shipments are delivered to secondary ports in Mainland China, before the products are sold to Chinese businessmen.

While there are a lot of negative developments and new challenges every week, there are also positive developments and trends. We can currently observe how an increasing number of consumer-facing businesses in Mainland China are adapting to their customers' preferences for more sustainability and environmental awareness.

---

[52] An old-growth forest (also known as primary forest or virgin forest) is a forest that has attained a high age without significant disturbance and therefore exhibits unique ecological features.
[53] This is around 1.110.000 square kilometres.

Additionally, the financial sector is quickly shifting towards a more sustainable approach as more and more research indicates reduced risk and equal (and sometimes better) financial performance with a stronger focus on environmental, social, and government approach. The Chinese are aiming at establishing a strong green financial system that drives ESG integration all across the country.

Throughout this book we have learned that while Chinese people might not like change, they do like innovation. One solution can come from more innovative and ESG focused financing in which public and private sector players work together in order to create a prosperous and sustainable investment environment. China's asset management industry is already proactively promoting ESG investing and sees the industry moving further into this direction. Additionally, we can see more and more regulatory action fostering a stronger integration of ESG. Looking ahead, ESG focused investment seems, while yet in its early stages, promising in China.

As the financing of companies will be linked closer to ESG factors, responsible investment will become increasingly aligned with economic restructuring and bottom-up ESG awareness. The demand for ESG will likely grow in the future and so will the need for companies to adapt. On the other hand, ESG investment is more in line with the ecological environmental protection requirements. Therefore, it is foreseeable that ESG investment will be increasingly implemented by China's local governments and domestic market players.

China's current president Xi Jinping has been consistent about his view that green policies are necessary in order "to protect the common home we live in". Therefore, China invested more than USD380 billion in many major sustainability programmes between Deng Xiaoping's early days in 1978 and 2015. Most of these investment took place in the second half. Surprisingly, this exceeds any other national sustainability programme.

In addition to that, on the more commercial side of sustainability, China is already producing cutting edge solar technology, offering low-carbon transportation, carbon trading, and an increasing circular economy.

The situation is still bad however. China accounts for nearly one-quarter of the world's non-natural emissions which makes it the second-largest producer of greenhouse gases after the US. And despite the fact that some large showcase cities such as Beijing or Shanghai are becoming less polluted and cleaner, Tier 2, Tier 3, and rural areas of China are still way behind western standards and often end up as waste yards for our consumption driven society. The situation gets worse if we consider that identifying a solution is oftentimes easier than actually implementing it. In theory, everybody wants to be more sustainable. But not everybody wants or is able to pay the price.

We can thus conclude that China is both a culprit and a victim when looking at environmental issues and sustainability. At the end, the lack of alternatives will force China to manage its resources based on recycling, conservation, and clean fuels – a trend we can already observe.

On a similar note we can expect that ESG investment will become an increasingly mainstream investment concept in China with an increasing variety in products, growing support from investors and growing demand from clients. Therefore, it is likely to see it become a driving force in the sustainable development of China and it's connected markets.

And while many benefits come with a stronger focus on sustainability, some expect that the cost of implementing such a strategy would seriously erode the country's industrial competitiveness. In the end, only time will tell.

# FOREIGN INVESTMENT IN CHINA

# 外资

When foreigners come to China, they oftentimes come transfixed by the size, scale and the idea that China, now open to the rest of the world, waits to be conquered. What they don't have in mind is that China is actually not awaiting them. This however does not matter to them once they learn that China has more than 1.4 billion citizen. What they forget is how diverse the country is. China is more diverse than many western countries and a market of 1.4 billion people breaks down fast into smaller and smaller segments. Not long after they arrive, they have to watch how the markets they hoped for gets sliced and diced into smaller pieces. The small market that is willing to buy their products is oftentimes hard to reach due to a multitude of layers of local protectionism, language barriers, and cultural differences.

When a new market is established domestic competition is oftentimes the first to reach the customer and better at communication, taking away that crucial first-mover advantage. While doing business in Asia is becoming easier, and especially in China after its opening-up policy, it is still far from being an easily reachable and accessible marketplace.

No doubt, China is working on further opening-up its economy and is aiming more and more for high-quality development. One way is making it easier to do business in China, another is to make foreign investment into China easier. It is likely that we will see China continue to widen market access for foreign investment as it not only helps China to develop but also to overcome existing challenges. To do this, it is important that China, when opening-up further, creates a business-friendly environment and protects the rights and interest of foreign investors.

We can easily see how China's economy is currently in a transition from a phase of rapid growth, that followed Deng Xiaoping's policies, to a phase that is focused on more high-quality development. Therefore, it is necessary, that China further increases its openness to gain not only profit from joint venture operations but to also to be more integrated in a globalised system. Xi Jinping and his team understand that in an era that is dominated by economic globalisation, China too should open its doors further, but instead of rushing they should rather cross the river by feeling the stones[54], as Deng Xiaoping once said.

China still needs to foster a better businesses and investment environment in order to widen market access for foreign players and thus attract foreign investment, which in return will help the country to innovate and move further into a high-quality economy.

Part of this foreign money comes in form of so called foreign direct investment (FDI). Foreign investment can be seen as an important driver of the economy that is able to help increase structural change across almost all sectors. Foreign investments can further help to create jobs and to introduce efficient production and management practices used abroad and thus positively contribute to an economy.

---

[54] Which translates to 摸着石头过河 in Chinese.

Furthermore, previously conducted research assumes a positive effect of investments coming from abroad on the overall gross domestic product. Foreign direct investment mainly focuses on business operations in the country with a direct controlling interest. Controlling interest suggest that the investor aims to gain an effective voice in the management of the enterprise. This effective voice usually means that investments are above a 10% threshold. On the other hand, foreign portfolio investment (FPI) focuses on financial assets, which, in contrast to direct investment, do not come with direct ownership rights.

Another benefit of foreign direct investments is a technology spill overs between companies, which tends to make organizational practices more efficient. FDI tends to improve the employment rate, which further increases the output at the macroeconomic level. This in return leads to an increase in income, which leads to more consumption of goods and services.

China's foreign direct investment (FDI) grew 6.8 percent year-on-year to around ¥370bn (USD53bn) in the first five months of 2019, according to data from the Chinese Ministry of Commerce.

In an recent report by the United Nations, China was ranked behind the United States as the world's second-largest recipient of foreign investment. This makes China the biggest recipient of foreign investment in Asia, before Hong Kong, accounting for more than 10 percent of total foreign direct investment.

Furthermore, when looking at ease-of-doing-business, China ranks 46th out of 190 countries in 2018. However, China's economy was still ranked second most attractive for multinational companies for 2017 to 2019, with the United States ranking first. It's the dream of size and scale that makes them comes, as they are still full of eagerness to conquer this 1.4 billion people market.

China, is working hard on further liberalizing the country, and continues to establish free trade zones to connect itself more and more with the rest of the world and benefit from the ambitions of these multinational companies.

Despite the increasing trade tensions between China and the United States, more than 60.000 companies were established by foreign investors in 2018 alone. The country is recording more and more M&A megadeals that benefit the economy and receives an increasing amount of money inflows from developing countries in Asia, such as Indonesia, and developed countries, such as Germany.

In 2016, Apple made a USD 1 billion funding deal with China's Didi Chuxing, a company we got to know earlier in this book. Diageo, the company behind famous drinks like Guinness, Johnnie Walker, Captain Morgan, Gordon's, and China's Shui Jing Fang, acquired a majority stake in Sichuan Swellfun for USD 9 billion.

The high-tech sector especially profited from increasing inflow of FDI over the last few years. This inflow has been rising significantly in the past few years and currently account for around one third of all foreign direct investment. Korea's Samsung for example invested more than USD 7 billion to expand its production line of memory chips in China.

The biggest investor however was Hong Kong. Due to the benefits of easier access, Hong Kong is the largest investor in China. Singapore, the Virgin Islands, South Korea, Japan, the United States, the Cayman Islands, the Netherlands, and Germany are next in this long list.

The majority of the foreign inflows was in the space of manufacturing, computer services, real estate, retail trade, transportation, electricity, and construction. Clearly, the high-quality sectors that China wants to develop further.

With new reforms China is focusing on increasing the ease of doing business further in order to attract even more foreign investment. So far the country already improved the delivery of major FDI projects, reduced its import tariffs for high-quality sectors, and more importantly it streamlined the process of establishing FDI even further.

From a western perspective China is still an established base for low cost production, which, despite more competition from China's neighbours, makes it an attractive market for investors.

Generally speaking, there are a still a lot of advantages to doing business in China. One, despite the fact that markets are oftentimes more segmented than people expect, China still offers the largest internal market in the world with a potential customer base of around 1.4 billion people. Additionally, China has an extremely well-developed production sector with lots of know-how in manufacturing and heavy industry. Labour cost are still comparatively low in China which is another benefit of this country.

However, the grass is always greener on the other side and there are also disadvantages that can make it hard and frustrating for foreign investors to expand to China. One is the relatively young and still developing legal environment which still leads to unnecessary administrative complexity of a lot of processes. Furthermore, we cannot deny the still eminent lack of transparency in many areas and the existing corruption. Intellectual property rights protection is another issue that caused many firms to reconsider their investment in China as they see this as a threat to their work. An additional problem can be production overcapacity in several sectors that is caused by too many players benefiting from the same trends. Another disadvantage that we should mention is the cultural difference between western people and Chinese people that can not only cause problems in communications but also in effectively establishing a business in China. Oftentimes the middle management is underdeveloped and qualified workers are missing. Achieving a similar quality of management and production can take months if not years.

Therefore, to achieve real high-quality economic development, China needs to ease market restrictions on foreign investment further while at the same time maintaining its culture and multitude of existing advantages.

Over the last few years the Chinese government has created numerous free-trade zones that allow for tax exemptions, tax incentives or other benefits to allow for overseas capital to find an easier way into the country. China has currently 5 special economic zones and an additional 14 coastal cities that have special rights. The special zones are Shenzhen (which is located just across the border to Hong-Kong), Zhuhai (which is also in Guangdong province and close to Macau), Shantou, Xiamen and the beautiful island of Hainan. The 14 coastal cities are Dalian, Shanghai, Ningbo, Qinhuangdao, Wenzhou, Fuzhou, Guangzhou, Zhanjiang (also in the province of Guangdong), Beihai (in the autonomous region of Guangxi Zhuang), Tianjin, Yantai, Qingdao (the former German colony), Lianyungang, and Nantong. Unlike the 5 special zones, who were seen as underdeveloped these coastal cities were already existing and key industrial centres in China, following the occupation of a multitude of foreign invaders. As you can see from the list, most of these cities were once occupied by the British or Japanese.

Generally speaking, the Chinese government is more restrictive than other countries with a similarly strong economy. China still hand-picks a lot of foreign investment and is still closed to FDI in a lot of key sectors. Additionally, state-owned companies are oftentimes seen as so called "national flagships" and protected by the government. The Chinese state might even demand forced technology transfer and its intellectual property protection system is weaker than most industrialised countries.

On the bright side, the government is moving towards restricting foreign investment in resource-intensive and highly polluting industries, as these are major drivers for environmental damages.

And while China continues to discourage foreign investment in some key sectors, for which China wants to transform its own domestic firms into globally competitive corporations, it still encourages additional foreign investment in high-end industries, technology, and environmental protection.

# CONCLUSION

After seeing China's past and learning about the different dynasties in the first part of this book we went on to learn about China's present in this Chapter. We learned about how different things work in China, how the past still influences the country and we guided the way to get a better understanding about where China might be heading.

In this chapter we learned how family obligation can be seen as a collection of personal characteristics that relate to the support and respect towards other family members. In the sense of family obligation, the family is seen as a big collective and a person belongs to this group and thus has responsibilities to contribute his part to the overall success of this group. The family can be as small as a few people that are closely related and as big as the whole of China. Thus, when making decisions, a person would take into account the needs of the family first – And similarly put the needs of China above that of other countries.

We also saw that following the increasing living standards all across the country, the demand for more housing in urban areas increased respectively. China's challenges are quite unique though, as the country had to face double digit growth for the majority of the last 20 years and deal with an enormous population size that can be hardly compared to any western country. Thus, over the past few years house prices grew rapidly to a point at which it became almost impossible for the majority of the population to buy their own property.

As a consequence we can observe an increasing disparity between urban and rural areas in terms of income and opportunity. While Deng Xiaoping weakened the migration control characteristics of the hukou system, disparities still remain, and removing this system seems very unlikely as it helped to control population size in the major cities. While the hukou system still discriminates against the rural population it might be the lesser of two evils.

To overcome many of the challenges that come with the rapid urbanisation China puts a strong emphasis on transportation in order to further boost economic growth and allow for a sustainable development. The biggest of these projects is the so-called Belt and Road Initiative (BRI) that we will talk about in the last part of this book. While China is genuinely profiting from the urban transportation networks that it developed over the past, a good transportation infrastructure by itself does probably not do enough. What is needed is a functioning supply and demand that can be built on these networks, turning them into successful projects that bring prosperity.

Another way to tackle the challenges that come with urbanisation and many more challenges of the 21$^{st}$ century, is to focus on more and more on technological advancements and innovation. We saw that while convenience is the new religion in China, innovation is its gospel. It is hard to deny that China will most likely have a major impact on the future of many technological improvements. The extreme wealth and easy access to data and information will likely lead to a new revolution of Internet of things (IoT), deep learning, and similar concepts.

Additionally, China's financial markets have been developing with a rapid pace since the late 1980s, following Deng Xiaoping's market reforms and the liberalization of the Chinese economy. Over the years the Chinese financial markets developed into sizable markets thanks to enhanced market infrastructures and a better legal and regulatory system.

China's payment system is an example of how technical innovation, urbanisation, and liberation of the financial markets all come together. We can most certainly assume that China is likely to keep this alternative payment system and built on it rather than to replace it. Additionally, foreign businesses serving Chinese retail customers will likely have to adopt to Chinese payment platforms. Thus, it is likely to assume that while China's payment system is expected to stay it is also likely to be further integrated into global payment systems.

With China's growth and advancement in technology comes also a duty to protect China as a country and that includes its environment. We have seen and learned that China is both a culprit and a victim when looking at environmental issues and sustainability. However, at the end of the day the lack of alternatives will force China to manage its resources based on recycling, conservation, and clean fuels, a trend we can already observe.

China is also working on further opening-up its economy and to continue its goal of a high-quality development. It is likely that China will continue to widen market access for foreign investment.

At current relative rates of growth, the size of the Chinese economy will match that of the US a few years before 2040. It can however be that China will grow old before it becomes rich. Before 2040 most of the children that grew up under Mao Zedong's population explosion will enter their retirement years. Even if the economy grows at 10 percent, it fails by a margin of several million to create the twenty-four million new jobs required each year. It seems unlikely that the birth rates in China will see a significant increase in the upcoming years as the pressure and additional burden is unlikely to change. This leaves China in a tight-grip and the leadership won't have much space in their decision making to ensure that employment crisis that is about to hit will be overcome.

We have seen that both Europe and the US are struggling and are not willing to accept that the global power distribution is changing to

China's favour. In the end, this will remain a major challenge for China in ensuring a prosperous future. China is reliant on foreign investment and trade and consequently vulnerable to protectionism. Many developments of the past were possible thanks to western goodwill and greed, but without it China will face new and drastic challenges.

Both, the United States and Europe find it increasingly hard to see the benefits of their engagement with China. Therefore, a key question to ask is how much the west will allow China to continue its growth and ascent without trouble. However, the western world is already dependent on China and one hand is feeding the other. Therefore, in order to get a better understanding of key developments, we will have a look at how the future of China might look like in the next part of this book.

# Third Part

## The Future of China

# THE FUTURE IS NOW

At this point we are coming closer to the finish line. So far we have looked at the history of China and the many dynasties that ruled the country up to the point where the People's Republic of China established a modern and communist China. We looked at concepts like Confucianism, Taoism, and Buddhism and in addition to that we looked at present day China. We saw the impact of some old traditions on this country and we learned how China differentiates itself from other countries. Over the last two chapters we paved the way for what can be China's future. Therefore, at this point it is time for us to take what we have learned so far and to risk a look ahead in time to see where China might be going.

In this section I will take an in-depth look at ten aspects that I chose to be interesting and relevant enough for understanding how China might develop in the next few years. Similar to the early chapters, I will talk about different aspects and include both the opinion of researchers, experts and my own. Like before, I urge you to make your own critical judgement and to stay curious.

The ten aspects that we are discussing in this part are first, innovation in China and how it will continue. Second, the urban trends and developments in China in the future. Third, the development of

China's currency. Fourth, the development of China into a control state. Fifth, the developments in the South China Sea and sixth, the developments in Tibet, Taiwan and Hong Kong. Seventh, the development of China into a global and local superpower. Eighth, a possible future for China's politics. Ninth, China's future role as peacekeeper and tenth, China's future as possible new number one.

Let's begin the last part of our journey.

# INNOVATION

—

We have learned so far that technology and new innovations have not only taken over everyday life but are also extremely important for China's future growth and success.

FDI inflows to the high-tech sector have been rising significantly and currently account for almost a third of total monetary inflow. This indicates two things. First, China is likely to turn into a leader in the high-tech sector driving innovation and thus attracting even more capital. Second, China is vulnerable since it is missing crucial diversification and due to the fact that it is still dependent on foreign investment and intellectual property.

China's citizens have developed a strong discipline for education and self-improvement along with a remarkable capacity for hard work, which is what the Chinese call "chī kǔ, 吃苦" or "eating bitterness". It is likely to be that this self-improvement goes hand in hand with more technological advancement, despite further protectionism from western nations. Recent technological trends and the growth of applications like WeChat and MoBike are an example of how innovation can happen domestically, despite increased tensions between nations. Therefore, we should not forget that despite increased friction with other states, China will have a major impact on future technological improvements and trends all around the world.

Sichuan opera is famous for the fast mask changing that is known as biàn liǎn (变脸) or "face changing". China's innovation and future can be beautifully captured with this image of quickly changing faces. China needs to transform itself in this quick way and wear a new face for the new challenges that it will be faced with in the future. The shift towards AI, Robotics, and stronger environmental protection are great examples of this as they offer potential answers to China's future problems of an aging population, environmental challenges, and the need for further high-quality growth. Therefore, Chinese companies are innovating like never before – a trend that is likely to continue.

When Germany talks about its strong economy and industry it oftentimes mentions the so called "hidden champions", a term that is used to describe small, highly specialized world-market leaders. This term of "hidden champions" is also applicable to China which is producing more and more world-market leaders in many fields of AI, Robotics and Industrial areas.

With Chinese companies moving up from low-end market segments to high-quality areas the implications for foreign companies are drastic. The competition is no longer on two different levels but between two equals (only that one might be seen as more equal as the other by the Chinese government). Thus, foreign companies who dream of selling their products to a broad Chinese market but are at the same time in fear of losing their intellectual property will have to learn that in the future they might be the ones that need to learn from the Chinese players and that they do not offer any more competitive advantage compared to their Chinese counterpart.

While a lot of people are sceptical about China's ability to develop a sustainable environment for innovation, due to its political ecosystem, China developed enough over the past few years to support a sustainable development and has proven them wrong.

Decades and years of foreign direct and indirect investment have allowed China to develop into a manufacturing superpower that is not only sustainable in providing and developing products but also able to innovate from their current state. China is rich in technological know-how and is able to provide skilled workers that can substitute foreign management and experts. This can be read as a warning to foreign companies that believe that they can offer superior products in the future to Chinese customers without innovating themselves. It is a race between who is innovating faster, which country is creating a better environment for innovation, and which companies are able to retain the smartest people.

China's many examples of innovation are visible in many areas, ranging from internet companies to software, telecommunication to fintech and artificial intelligence. The space in-between isn't empty though but rather filled with even more examples of innovation in forms of new materials or high-end equipment.

China's domestically grown companies like Tencent, Baidu, Alibaba, or Huawei are not only known outside their homeland but leading innovation all over the world and offering superior solutions that many western companies struggle to match. Over the course of a long and eventful history, China has managed to reach a point where it is able to do what it can do best: Innovate. With innovations like the compass, printing, gunpower and others, China is now at a point where it will lead a new wave of revolution.

The question is whether the west will be able to compete with China and how it will react, if it is faced with Chinese competition that is able to have a fair fight against names like Alphabet and Amazon. At the end of the day, despite many arguing that China played an unfair game in the past, it was neither an unfair advantage nor the vast amounts of invested capital that made China's tech companies what they are today. Instead, it is the strong focus on using data to understand the customers. And I mean really understand them. It is this user-focused approach and the view that innovation is healthy that made Chinese businesses successful.

If this wouldn't be enough, government initiatives such as "Made in China 2025[55]" are designed to help the tech sector to develop further and to increase ideas-driven innovation. China is already the second largest investor in AI enterprises (after the United States) and has high ambitions to be the number one by 2030.

In the face of the US-China rivalry, Made in China 2025, is already seen as the real threat to the US leadership that in the eyes of the US Government can still be stopped by stronger protectionism against China.

At the end of the day, it is likely that the rivalry between the US and China will deepen as to who is the leader in technology and the real innovative power in the world. While both can exist next to each other, it is likely that neither wants to share the title with the other.

On another note, it is important for China to maintain healthy development of its industrial and technology sector in the future and to continue deepening reforms and to allow for a further opening-up in order to make the domestic companies world-leaders in their field and allow for them to unfold their full potential.

---

[55] Made in China 2025 is a strategic plan by the Chinese government which is aimed at moving away from the predominant production of cheap products towards higher quality products and services that are locally sourced. The aim is to achieve independence from foreign suppliers for such products and services.

# URBANIZATION

二

U rbanization is what we know as the growth in the proportion of a population living in urban areas. China included, it is one of the major social changes sweeping over the globe. Data indicates that urban population is growing at a faster rate than the rate of total population growth. Already, more than 3 billion people, so almost half of the world, are living in cities.

Data published by the Chinese Ministry of Construction, show that China's urbanization level increased from around 18% in 1978 to around 40% in 2003 and around 58% in 2017. It is expected, that China's urbanization will continue, with the urbanization ratio reaching more than 70% by the year 2035. And while the percentage growth rate of urbanization is decreasing the ratio will constantly increase, with cities allowing for better employment and not only better transportation, housing, and infrastructure, but also the possibility of climbing the social ladder.

The Chinese government realised that in order to keep the economy growing, they need to further develop their urban network and allow for easy and efficient movement between them.

At a time where climate change is dominating the globe China is faced with a major task: It needs to further grow existing systems and plan ahead to make them resilient to new challenges that the changing climate is bringing. Therefore, many future projects are taking into account climate change, focusing on reducing disruption by possible future disasters. At the current rate, China's entire bus fleet is likely to be completely electric before the year 2025.

However, due to the fact that urbanization is strongly dependent on a steady and recurring supply of natural resources, including fresh water and land, China faces an intensified resource scarcity and the possibility for more environmental degradation in the future.

Another concept is the combination of technology and urbanization in so called "smart living" which China aims to develop further in the coming years. Beijing, Shanghai and Shenzhen are the leaders in China's urban innovation and will function as working examples for the many second tier cities that will follow.

One current and future concept that the Chinese government will develop further is that of urban cluster, in which multiple cities will come together. Two well-known examples are the "Jing-Jin-Ji" cities Beijing, Tianjin, and Hebei and the Yangtze Delta cluster around Shanghai. The idea is that these integrated clusters will alleviate pressure on overcrowded cities like Beijing and Shanghai.

It is likely that China's urban morphology will continue to develop into an urban agglomeration within the next 15 years. These areas will in return offer and support important functions of modern cities, including a strong industrial and technology sector, opportunities in education, and much more. Small- and medium-sized cities on the other hand will function as support for the cities and offer everything from manufacturing to heavy-industry.

These urban clusters will also get more infrastructure development to allow for a fast and easy commute. Second- and third-tier cities will open new universities that further help to manage the increasing population in the first-tier cities. Otherwise, massive populations moving to the leading cities in the country will continue to put additional pressure on employment and other related issues.

It is estimated that China has a migrant population in its cities that exceeds 220 million. This population largely consist of people that came from the most rural parts of the country in search for a better life and employment in the cities. These migrant worker are oftentimes undereducated and extremely poor.

At the end of the day we have to accept that most of the urbanization that we saw over the last 40 years did not happen because the government planned for it but because the economy asked for it. The hukou system, which we learned about earlier, helped to slow down this process, but it is still not able to stop it. China's agglomeration areas are one way to cope with this fast and unplanned urbanisation.

Another way is to start from scratch. Oftentimes already existing infrastructure is restricting the development of China's megacities and are not designed for the urbanization and transportation challenges, that China is facing in the 21$^{st}$ century. China's modern cities like Shenzhen are oftentimes dominated by market dynamics, offering efficient and resilient commuting opportunities and residential areas. They offer malls and parks and a very different dynamic than cities like Beijing.

In Beijing people are faced with numerous historical traditions and restrictions and while population size is driving the need for innovation and change, it is oftentimes the urban design that is the biggest challenge. One possible solution would be to create a planed-capital similar to Malaysia, Myanmar, and other Asian countries. In fact, at this point nothing but low priority speaks against such a development in the future.

Urbanisation in China is not fair and it likely stay unfair for the foreseeable future. The relocation we looked at so far was always voluntarily. This however does not always have to be the case. China's older generation is oftentimes overwhelmed with the change and life in the cities and at the end of the day they don't adapt to the urban life that the government is envisioning for them. While China's urbanisation seems desirable at first, it also has its dark sides.

One thing is for sure, though. It is continuing and it is unavoidable. At the end, there won't be any other way to lift more people out of poverty without an increasing rate of urbanization. What we will need to watch in the future is how China's government is tackling this extremely demanding and important challenge.

# RENMINBI

三

China has high ambitions for its currency, the renminbi. Renminbi (人民币) means "the people's currency" and is better known by the name for its biggest unit, called yuan.

Every country dreams of a strong currency, some of being a reserve currency, others of being a global currency. As a matter of fact, there are a lot of benefits that come with having a reserve currency. Those countries that promote their currency to become a reserve currency oftentimes reap the benefits of it.

One of these benefits lies in pricing international contracts and with a reserve currency status China would be able to increase the volume of contracts that are priced in yuan. Additionally, given that China exports a lot of commodities like iron ore, crude oil, and soybeans, that are usually priced in US dollars it is exposed to volatility in the dollar value. A reserve currency status and the ability to price these commodities dominantly in yuan would help China to worry less about the developments in the value of the US dollar. A third benefit would lie in the fact that central banks are demanded to hold foreign exchange reserves. Giving the yuan a reserve currency status would increase the demand over-night. Furthermore, it would not only help to lower the interest rates for those bonds that are denominated in yuan but also lower the borrowing costs of many Chinese export companies.

In its early days, after joining the World Trade Organization in 2001, foreign investors were for the first time allowed to buy yuan-denominated stocks. These stocks are the A-shares we learned about earlier in this book. A few years later, around 2005, the yuan's peg was initially dropped but put back in place around 2008 to protect China from the consequences of the US triggered financial crisis. Around 2010 China overtook Japan's economy as the world largest.

A few years later, following Xi Jinping's economic reforms the International Monetary Fund (IMF) awarded the yuan a reserve currency status in late 2015. This not only gave China the above-mentioned advantages but also helped to raise China's position in relation to the United States. Following the IMF's upgrade in 2015 the yuan was added to the IMF's special drawing rights basket in 2016, an exclusive club that includes the US dollar, the Euro, the Japanese yen, the British pound, and now the Chinese yuan.

The decision of the IMF didn't come as a surprise, though, as the yuan's popularity grew since the early days of China's reform and opening-up. Under Xi Jinping it became the fourth most-used currency in the world in 2015.

China's leaders are working hard to make it easier to trade the yuan in foreign exchange markets and in this spirit they continue to open China's markets. One of the developments that is still needed is the creation of more trust, similar to the US financial system. In addition to that, the Chinese government needs to further develop the transparency of its financial markets in order to allow for more stability and reliability. Stability, transparency, trust, and a strong economy are just a few reasons why the US dollar is the current world's reserve currency and not any other.

However, at this point the Chinese yuan is still far from being the world's reserve currency. The same holds for being Asia's reserve currency since China's renminbi is not significantly used outside the borders of Mainland China. China still has strong restrictions on buying and selling its currency and while this helps to keep out bad capital it also keeps out good capital. Most importantly, though, it helped China to keep its products comparatively cheap.

In order to continue its strong growth, China needs to continue to fuel its economy. One way to do so is by further loosening the grip around the renminbi and by allowing markets to work without too much government intervention. This should in return help to attract foreign portfolio investment and allow for new foreign money to find its way into the hands of Chinese companies.

If you payed attention to China over the last few years you could observe that China is also trying to further promote its currency abroad. Predominantly, this is happening in China's neighbouring countries and those countries that become increasingly involved in the Belt and Road Initiative. While this is helping China by attracting new money, it is also allowing for more volatility and thus less stability of China's financial markets.

We saw this newly introduced instability impacting China's currency for the first time in August 2015, when the currency got devalued. As a response, Chinese authorities focused again on supporting the currency, which effectively cost them more than USD 1 trillion by 2017. China again tightened its rules on money leaving the country and with the currency continuing to strengthen into 2018 China's economy recovered. Looking ahead, while still assuming strong Chinese control in the background, it is likely to expect that China's grip is loosening further as the country will need to ensure foreign capital flowing into the country going forward. Thus, market forces will again have a bigger impact on the exchange rates. And while I believe this to be the genuine case, I also believe that there is still a long way to go in China's journey to internationalize its currency.

Currently, when looking at the volume of world trade, we can see that China only accounts for about 10 percent. However, while this is the case only around 2 percent of the global payments are actually made in yuan. One initiative that might change this very soon is the "Belt and Road Initiative". Xi Jinping already pledged more than 100 billion yuan of funding and with China's currency in the reserves of central banks most of the payments can be expected to be made in this currency. Furthermore, China's leaders are working on making the yuan convertible by the end of 2020. This however, will leave China again in a more vulnerable position and exposed to money flows that could negatively impact the economy.

Taking into account that China is already challenging the US on the economic front, it is understandable, that the US are now afraid that China will do something similar with its currency and challenge the dominance of the US dollar as main reserve currency around the world. If China's currency would be used more widely around the world China's influence in setting prices of commodities ranging from oil to iron ore would get easier and domestic Chinese companies would find it easier to do business abroad, dictating the terms of business.

However, while it is undeniable that China wants to further integrate into global markets, it is hard to see that China indeed can and wants to challenge the US as dominant currency at this point in time or in the near future. A good reminder of seeing the dominance of the United States can actually be found in Asia itself. When looking at the emerging economies across Asia you can see that the majority of them still anchor their currencies to the US dollar rather than the Chinese renminbi. The same holds when looking at the currencies that Asian countries use to borrow money. We can disregard other currencies such as the Euro or the Pound since only a marginal amount of emerging market debt is denominated in those currencies. At the end of the day, when it boils down to the dominant global currency that is used for reserves central banks, the dollar is unrivalled and is likely to stay unrivalled for the near future.

In order to better understand the struggles that China's currency is facing, it is useful to also get a better understanding about why the US dollar is so dominant around the world. One key reason is the position of the US economy and the strong trading activity that the US financial system has to offer. Another key reason why the US currency is so dominant compared to others was the previously mentioned weakness of China's financial system — its transparency. It is this transparency that makes the US financial system credible and predictable. With the Federal Reserve System the United States are able to create credibility around its monetary policy which makes it a safe-haven for those who are afraid of devaluation. Furthermore, the US economy is able to work despite trade deficits.

Of course there is also another factor and that is simply convenience and cost saving when trading in US dollar compared to Chinese yuan. Considering that already the majority of reserves is in US dollars, it could takes years, if not decades for those reserves to shift into another currency. Thus, at the end of the day it is likely that the US dollar will remain the dominant global reserve currency.

China, despite its now relatively strong economy, still has a long way to go. Its currency does not yet float freely, local financial markets are still strongly regulated and hard to access for foreign investors and China's monetary policy is a black box for most. It is necessary, that China allows market forces to play a bigger role in determining the true value of its currency. This however is easier said than done. Just "simply" opening the capital accounts to foreign investors would require a complete change of the financial system.

Considering the many challenges that China is facing at the moment, now might not be the best time to tackle these changes. China is currently faced with an enormous amount of domestic debt and the government works hard to keep the system working.

Thus, while China's yuan is now finally included in the exclusive list of reserve asset currencies, the country still has a lot of catching up to do. Before it can improve the credibility of its financial markets, it first has to overcome the existing debt challenge.

As for now, the yuan is still far from being a global reserve currency. Chinese currencies and government bonds are held to a minimum but far from becoming a top-notch investment and a high-quality reserve asset like the US dollar. Once China overcomes these challenges, there is a gap waiting for the country to be filled. As for now, it is time for China to build on the existing developments.

# CONTROL STATE

四

M any Chinese live a life that is very different to that of western people. China is an enormously large country and still has a massive number of low income and poorly educated citizens that are spread from the west to the far east of the country. In addition to that, despite recent changes, corruption is still present in China and the civil society and in some areas China can still not hold up to western standards.

Applying well known concepts like personal and political freedom to these ground rules is seen as potentially disrupting and high-level politicians fear that simply copying western concepts will lead the country into chaos. As a consequence, China is looking for other ways to manage its 1.4 billion people and make sure that the country will continue its success stories of the last few decades. China wants to become a strong, respected, and wealthy nation that is unified in its centre and able to hold up a nationalistic pride that is led by a government that has the interest of the people in mind. China's lessons from the past have shown that western concepts have little to offer and might be harder to apply than people believe without causing chaos and unrest in the country. China is not inclined to endorse a western, liberal democratic, political system in which power would be divided and decisions oftentimes only applicable in the short-term.

However, more and more Chinese, especially the more educated urban class that usually lived abroad for an extended period of time, are changing their beliefs gradually. It is thus easy to make the mistake to see them as a representation of the overall country.

For most Chinese, the western political and social models still have little to offer. They mainly see the tools needed for advancements in concepts like achieving economic prosperity and the development into a global power - two key characteristics that are worth studying in more detail.

One way to make sure everything goes as planned is by censoring what people can say, making sure that it is the communication of the ruling party that is reaching the people and not an independent interpretation that might cause unrest in the country. Censorship in the People's Republic of China is implemented and mandated by the ruling party and focuses on censoring content for political reasons in order to maintain control over the communication of news. And while the right to free speech is clearly impacted and restricted, the Chinese government sticks by its argument that it has the legal right to control the internet's content within its territory and that their censorship rule clearly doesn't impact the right to free speech. This approach intensified once Xi Jinping became the General Sectary of the Communist Party.

Up until today the government maintains censorship over all media that reaches a wide audience. Applications like WeChat are designed to limit the reach of post and to make sure that the government stays ahead when it comes to demonstrations or negative news. The control reaches from print media all the way to television, news, theatre, film, video games, to the internet as a whole. And while censoring gets more difficult with new technologies emerging the Chinese government is still able to exercise control over its citizens with almost unlimited access to uncensored information with the use of an internal documentation system.

The organization "Reporters Without Borders" repeatedly ranks China's press freedom as "very serious", giving the country the worst possible ranking. The Chinese government filters out unwelcomed views and censors views that are "harming the system". Most of the major media outlets across the country receive guidance from the Chinese Department of Propaganda (Yes, it is really called like that!) on what is politically acceptable and thus approved by the ruling party.

The range of content that is banned is wide ranging. The Chinese government has strong bans on independence movements in Tibet and Taiwan and demonstrations in its western province Xinjiang. I was still in Shenzhen when the protest in Hong Kong started and despite reading about them early on in western and Hong Kongnese newspapers, Chinese newspapers did not report on it until it became too big to be ignored. Funnily, the ruling partly said itself that the domestic media must "ensure that the party and government do not become the targets of focus on criticism".

With leading technology companies such as Tencent and Baidu, and fast improvements in information technology in the last few years, the Communist party has reached an inflection point where it can use exactly this technology to further promote propaganda and the agenda of the communist party. Thus, going forward we will likely see that these trends continue and that China's propaganda work is not only intensifying but also reaching new areas of life that it did not touch before.

At the end of the day many western politicians and analyst will likely be proven wrong. While they oftentimes only watch from their stand point, and assume that China will see more political freedoms going forward, the opposite is happening. China became more and more prosperous over the years, but instead of demanding political freedom, the Chinese citizens put more of their trust into the one-party rule that helped their social ascent in the first place. Over the last few years we could observe how Xi Jinping consolidated power, while the income levels of most cities grew over the same period.

The long assumed western assumption that prosperity stirs democratization seems not to work for China, a country that seems to go against the grain. As for now, there is little reason to see this changing in the near-term as maintaining a control state is also important for internal security. And with many in fear to speak out it will be impossible to make reliable predictions from the outside as we don't know how many Chinese might disapprove of the current system.

# EAST & SOUTH CHINA SEA

五

A very different topic is that about the future of the East and South China Sea. Both seas, the East China Sea and the South China Sea form the China Sea. As you have already learned, the South China Sea is bounded on the west by the Asian mainland consisting of Vietnam, Cambodia, Laos, Thailand, Malaysia, and Singapore. It is bound on the south by a rise in the seabed between Sumatra and Borneo, and on the east by Borneo, the Philippines, and Taiwan. The sea's northern boundary extends from the northernmost point of Taiwan to the coast of Fujian province in China. It covers an area of more than 1,420,000 square miles (around 3,685,000 square km) which makes it the largest marginal sea of the western Pacific. Looking at it in more detail you can see numerous rivers flowing into the South China Sea, making it a key area for maritime transportation. To name just a few, we have those that form the Pearl River Delta, the Xi river, the Red and Mekong river in Vietnam and many more.

When talking about the South China Sea we should not make the mistake to forget about the East China Sea. The East China Sea extends north-eastward from the South China Sea and is bounded on the west by the Chinese mainland and on the east by the Ryukyu Islands chain, which consist out of Japan's southernmost main island, and South Korea's Cheju Island. The East China Sea has the size of about 290,000 square miles (thus around 750,000 square km).

Both seas are currently impacted by heavy fishing and fish from the South China Sea provide as much as 50 percent of the animal protein consumed along the densely populated coast of Southeast Asia. Most of the fishing is done by small local boats and tuna, mackerel, shrimp, sardines, and shellfish are the main resources that are harvested.

More interesting maybe is the fact that both petroleum, and natural gas deposits have been discovered under the sea's continental shelf. And as you can assume, these discoveries (amongst other things) have led to increasing disputes between the bordering countries over the control of areas with potentially exploitable resources. With China's growing demand in Oil & Gas it is likely that we will see their dominance in this region growing as they would want to assure that they have access to the resources.

Additionally, both seas are important and strategic shipping routes. On the one hand we have the South China Sea, with the Strait of Malacca – the major transport route that connects the Pacific with the Indian ocean. More than 45% of worldwide transnational exchange is transported across it, making it one of the most important transportation paths in the world. On the other hand, we have the strategic routes that connect southern countries to Japan and other important ports in the north. The most important ports in the East China Sea are the Port of Shanghai in China, the world's busiest container port with more than 29 million twenty-foot equivalent units[56] (TEUs), and the Nagasaki port in Japan.

---

[56] The twenty-foot equivalent unit is an unit measure of a cargo capacity and used to describe the capacity of container ships and terminals.

A clash between the different states, connected through the South China Sea, would likely have a negative impact on worldwide trade and negatively impact all countries involved. Over the years the South China Sea and the Paracel and Spratly Islands within this area, turned into a new key driver for conflicts between Brunei, China, Malaysia, the Philippines, Taiwan, and Vietnam. All of them want a piece of the rich oil and gas reserves in this area and control over important trade points.

China went so far to create more than eight million square meters of human-manufactured islands in the South China Sea to underline its claim on the geopolitically important maritime area.

Once you understand that the South China Sea is more than just a maritime fishing space, but a crucial geopolitical location, you can understand better why China has such interest in claiming it as Chinese territory. Around 80% of Japans and more than 70% of Taiwan's oil and crude material imports come across the South China Sea, transported by gigantic boats, loaded with supplies of raw petroleum, liquid gas, coal, and iron metal. Controlling these supplies gives China tight control over both these countries without any direct interaction. By owning the supply chain, China's dominance and control in Asia is growing. Due to projects like the Belt and Road Initiative, it is expected to become the leading economy in Asia.

Taking all this into account it is likely to assume that China's grip on the South China Sea and it claims will continue with more artificial islands manifesting China's dominance. The South China Sea is of too much strategic importance to do anything else.

China still claims the greatest part of the South China Sea and with its already dominant position there is only little left for countries like the Philippines and Brunei. China says to have the longest historical claim, dating back to the early Han dynasty. However, it hasn't been until around the 15th century that Chinese historians mentioned the Spratly Islands. The first official claim over the Paracel Islands dates back to around 1876 which doesn't give these claims much foundation.

After the downfall of the Qing dynasty the Republic of China lost some control over the South China Sea and some of its Islands went to Japan and other countries.

Approaching the end of the 20th century China started to increase it claims, and changed it political stance to enforce this claim around the South China Sea. Around this time the now famous nine-dashed map was first released[57]. Within this nine-dashed line is around 90% of the South China Sea, including the island of Taiwan. However, despite the publication of the nine-dashed map, China has not yet filed for a formal and specifically defined claim and might not want to do so soon as not to spike global and Asian anger. Instead, China is doing what it does best and is instead changing things by acting in an indirect way rather than by using words or direct confrontation, leaving behind an already painted picture.

Many people raised concerns, that under the United Nations Convention on the Law of the Sea (UNCLOS) there is no credible basis for China to claim most of the South China Sea. The international community is rejecting historical rights as a credible reason. Many countries, including the Philippines and Vietnam do not accept China's claim of the South China Sea and refer to the rules set by the UNCLOS. It is unlikely at this point that this opinion will change and that China's claim on the South China Sea will be accepted by the international community anytime soon – Another reason no the make this claim formal.

However, due to the increasing speed at which China is building massive islands in the middle of the South China Sea, it becomes harder for many of the neighbouring nations to rely on protection that is simply based on the distance from mainland China. And while Chinese efforts are countered by alternate forces, China's economic strength and military dominance in the region puts China at a crucial

---

[57] The nine-dashed map was first released in 1947. It refers to the demarcation line that is used by the People's Republic of China for their claims of major parts of the South China Sea. Starting at the southern Chinese mainland, the u-shaped nine-dashed line extends downwards along the shores of the Philippines and Vietnam far away from the Chinese mainland all the way to the Malaysian coast.

advantage. China has still one of the fastest growing economies in the world. And with an increase in growth finally came an increase in China's navy and container ship fleet, making it one of the biggest and most important in the world. The old days of Zheng He seem long over and China is now in a position where the former maritime humiliation seems unimaginable. China is promoting its shipbuilder industry with huge amounts of subsidies and China's control over more than 52 important seaports. It is building islands in the South China Sea and uses them as strategic military bases. At the end of the day it will be this silent ascent to power that will – while maybe not legally defined – give China the control over the South China Sea that it is looking for.

# INTEGRATION

T his chapter tries to answer what the future might hold for Tibet, Taiwan and Hong Kong in relation to China.

If you recall, Tibet was conquered during the period of the Qing dynasty making it officially part of the country. During the 20th century, with the fall of the Qing empire Tibet, for the first time, regained some degree of independence again. However, the question if Tibet, Taiwan, or Hong Kong belong to China is not straight forward to answer because there is no black and white answer.

While historically Tibet belong to China during the period of the Qing, it was independent during the time of the Republic of China after the British demanded the separation between Tibet and China. Interestingly, the British still had their colony in India and having an independent Tibet helped to create some distance to China. Practically speaking re-entering Tibet could be seen as an imperialistic move from China. However, it is worth pointing out again that this was something most of the "democratic" colonial powers did for decades without calling it military conquest but instead spread of "civilisation" or "prosperity". Considering the forced independence, the Chinese might not have a perfectly legitimate claim on Tibet, but saying they would have no claim at all is also wrong. Whatever your view on this is, judging too fast in this matter might be the wrong thing to do as China only left Tibet due to the demands of the British in the first place.

More recently, since 1950, Tibet has been ruled by the Communist Party of the People's Republic of China. Gaining power and momentum China decided to state its claim on Tibet after the second world war and soon claimed that Tibet had always been a part of the country, never having been a sovereign state.

This of course holds against the fact that Tibet, which is located on a remote plateau in the Himalayan Mountain range, for many hundreds of years was ruled by a King out of Lhasa, the capital of the country. After the Tibetan Empire was established it engaged in multiple cultural exchanges. During that time, it was the Chinese occupation that introduced Buddhism to this remote plateau. Once the Silk Road was established, outsiders connected more and more with Tibet through the trade along this long economic corridor. In the past the Chinese have always been involved in Tibet's politics and early Chinese records date back to around 208 AD. It is due to these records that, similar to the South China Sea, China is making claims on past events.

Going forward it is hard to imagine anything else for Tibet but more economic and social integration with China. This, would turn the table as it would now be a buffer to keep America and India further away from China. However, a first step for China is to annex Tawang, which might be the next birthplace of the Dalai Lama. Only by doing so will China be able to fully subdue Tibet and drive a further integration of this previously Chinese territory.

China's relation to Taiwan is quite different. Most of Taiwan's citizen have Chinese roots due to the retreat of China's nationalist in the attempt to escape the anger of the rising Communist party. By the end of the civil war almost two million nationalists lived in Taiwan.

As a matter of fact, in the early days the new government of Taiwan almost perfectly resembled the Chinese government before the civil war.

Unlike Tibet, Taiwan cannot neglect its historical roots it was built on. The People's Republic of China views the island as a province and while Taiwan is not neglecting this, over the years it grew its wish for more independence.

Up until today both China and Taiwan have a fragile relationship with each other with China being clearly the stronger party of both. However, up until today Beijing and Taipei disagree on the island's status.

The idea that there is only "One China" and that Taiwan is without a doubt part of China dates back to 1992. In 1992 both the Chinese Communist Party and the Kuomintang, the ruling political party of Taiwan, agreed on the fact that there is only "One China". Different interpretations of these two words allowed Taiwan to be semi-independent so far with its own governing body.

However, despite this earlier understanding, Taiwan drifted further and further apart from the Mainland over the years. So far that Taiwan's current president, Tsai Ing-wen, the leader of the Democratic Progressive Party, has refused to speak about the 1992 consensus.

Going back all the way to the year 1979 we can see how the United States and Jimmy Carter, the US president at that time, agreed that there is only one China and that Taiwan is part of China. As a consequence, the United States decided to terminate its diplomatic relations with the Taiwanese government. Despite this, the United States Congress also passed the so-called Taiwan Relations Act in which it is committed to the island's security and safety.

Up until today this relationship is extremely important for both Taiwan and the United States. Taiwan can feel relatively safe and independent thanks to the presence of US forces. The United States on the other hand needs Taiwan. For the US, a presence in Taiwan is crucial for their position in the Asia-Pacific region. Without any presence in this region the United States might be at risk of losing the right to call themselves a "world power".

Fast forward to 2016, the year Tsai Ing-wen, got elected, president Xi Jinping announced that China will not allow for any separatist path and any form of Taiwan's independence. He emphasized that Taiwan needs to adhere to the "One China" principle.

Looking ahead to what the future might hold for Taiwan it is important to be aware of the crucial role that Taiwan is playing for both the US and China.

If China would deem its strategy of economic integration as a driver of political reunification as failed, there are only little alternatives left and China may try a more aggressive approach towards Taiwan. The US however will be in a position where their response will decide whether its words have credibility or not.

At this point China has already changed its balance in relation to Taiwan in almost all aspects, including military and economic power. Thus, it might be that the leadership in Beijing soon sees its economic and military dominance as a force that can drive Taiwan into unification.

In order to achieve a reunification with Taiwan, Beijing will need to reconcile the deep biases between the Chinese and Taiwanese governments. Within Taiwan, there is the fear that once Beijing achieved a reunification with Taiwan, it will impose communist rules on the small southern island. It is hard to neglect the differences between the nationalist government in Taiwan and Beijing, and that after decades of their "war of words" most Taiwanese would likely hope for the current status to remain for the time being.

Xi Jinping, however, is following Deng Xiaoping's approach so far in seeing Taiwan and China as "one country with two systems".

The stakes are high and China is in a position where it can only allow little mistakes. Therefore, a possible outcome might be that the status quo continues for an unspecified period of time in which China can focus on growing its economy and avoiding the middle-income trap, while Taiwan will have more time to move further away from China.

The political stand-off will continue and political compromises on both sides of the cross-strait. At the end of the day and in the face of increasing Chinese political, diplomatic, economic and military pressure, Taiwan's future appears ever more uncertain.

And despite that it might yet not be enough to convince Taiwan to give up it's almost independence. The United States is a critical ally that has as much interest in Taiwan's independence as the country itself. Thus, while there is clearly more uncertainty in East Asia and the risk are higher, Taiwan's chances of independence have not yet diminished.

Taiwan and Hong Kong can be compared in many ways. Taiwan is fully democratic and Hong Kong semi-democratic, bot states are rooted in Confucianism and they are both using the same Chinese language. However, it is worth to look at Hong Kong separately at this point.

In the 1980s both, the United Kingdom and the People's Republic of China, agreed on returning Hong Kong to Chinese sovereignty in 1997, under the "one country, two systems" agreement. This agreement transfers the sovereignty of Hong Kong from the British back to the China. Under the terms of the agreement, Hong Kong will become a "Special Administrative Region" which will retain a high degree of autonomy for a period of fifty years.

Soon after this, the Asian Financial Crisis hit the world and to protect Hong Kong's economy the People's Republic of China agreed to the "Economic Partnership Arrangement" (CEPA) in 2003. The idea was to close the gap between both economies further, increase free trade and introduce more Chinese tourist to Hong Kong.

Since the introduction of CEPA in 2003, Hong Kong became more and more dependent on Chinese capital and tourist. In 2016 alone, more than 42 million Mainland Chinese visited Hong Kong. This is more than six times the city's population. In addition to that, new Chinese immigrant, using a so called "one-way permit" account for around 1% of annual population growth in Hong Kong. Most of these immigrants are less skilled and in need of public housing. Going forward it is likely to assume, that despite ongoing protest the influx of immigrants will lead to a further acceleration in the city's housing problem.

Over the course of the last years we could see how an increased income gap and rising inequalities lead to a decline in trust towards the government. Especially vulnerable groups such as students, unemployed and worker in low-income jobs, drove an increase in the tension with the Mainland, assuming that an independent Hong Kong is in a better position to create growth and prosperity for future generations. Additionally, while in Taiwan the public can always impact the countries faith through elections and other democratic measures, these options are not available in Hong Kong. Instead, having no other alternatives at hand, we see how more and more people support radial political movements. Hong Kong has almost no impact on any of the integration-oriented policies. Thus, more and more younger people support radical propositions, protest or leave.

It is important to remember that Hong Kong doesn't even have its own elections for the leadership of the Peninsula. And while protest erupted in 2014, 2018 and are still ongoing, little change can be expected going forward.

In November 2019 we could see a wave of pro-democracy candidates winning seats in the district-level elections. Beijing is thus at a crucial point where it has to make a decision about the fate of Hong Kong. Since it always tried to promote the same "one country, two system" approach to Taiwan it is important for China to make sure that the divide between Hong Kong and China is not leading to the loss of the semi-autonomous region. We could already see how the violence in Hong Kong contributed to the victory of Tsai Ing-wen in Taiwan.

At this point, other than a potential international economic retaliation against China, there seem to be little consequences that China would need to face. It just seems that at the end, the Chinese will have the absolute control over the fate of Hong Kong. And while it seems to be in the best interest of both to maintain Hong Kong's system with as much stability as possible, this can also mean a stronger

Chinese influence to guarantee this stability. At this point it seems unlikely to imagine a politically independent and fully democratic Hong Kong. Hong Kong will be at the mercy of the People's Republic and it seems unlikely that Beijing will be willing to let go of this territory. Hong Kong has no choice but to be integrated further and become part of the People's Republic of China.

Of bigger interest is probably how this will affect Hong Kong and how Beijing would react to further and increased social unrest.

China seems to be in a position where it cannot allow to compromise further, since it might send the wrong signal to Taiwan. At this point, reunification with Taiwan will likely either occur as a result of a military conquest or substantial political change, and there is little reason at this point to assume the latter. While Taiwan will likely try to postpone a reunification as long as possible, China might not want to wait forever.

Similar to Taiwan, China might not want to wait until 2047 since Hong Kong might have drifted away too much by then. And while the People's Republic cannot just cut itself of from the rest of the world it might be willing to take some pain if it means that it can force a stronger hand on Hong Kong and its local affairs. It just comes with little surprise that China released blueprints on how it wants to tighten its grip on Hong Kong. The most recent plans include the creation of a Chinese led security agency and weakening of the local judiciary system are very likely just the first steps in further increasing the Chinese influence on Hong Kong.

To really understand the importance of the most recent developments we should understand what they mean. Up until now Hong Kong retained its own legal system and China guaranteed that until 2047 the Special Economic Region would keep a "high degree of autonomy". At this point there is little doubt that Chinese lawmakers will approve of further legislation that will result in China's increased influence over Hong Kong.

# EXPANSION

七

S oon after Mao Zedong died Deng Xiaoping enter the stage of Chinese politics and became the key figure in shaping the future of the country. In 1978 he took the stage and explained that China has to overcome its reluctance to learn from the developed world in order to be powerful and prosperous again. The only way to achieve this is by opening-up the country and modernizing the economy.

Soon after this speech China started to open-up its economy like announced and allowed for foreign capital to flow into the country through the implementation of so called special administrative regions (SARs).

The world changed again in 2013 when president Xi Jinping announced "One Belt, One Road" (一带一路), also known as the Belt and Road Initiative (BRI). The Belt and Road Initiative that we know today involves more than 70 countries and is a global development strategy led by the Chinese government, involving but not limited to infrastructure projects all over the world.

The project itself is enormous and the timeline set for the realization for most projects is longer than any other project, ranging from 2013 until the year 2049. In-between the Chinese government will conclude single milestones - the first being in 2021. The Belt and Road Initiative is so important for China's role in the world that it is seen as one of the most active foreign policies strategies Beijing ever announced. It symbolises a change from a China that is bound by environmental factors to a China that is leading and shaping its environment rather than adopting to it.

In the long-run, spinning a spider web into other countries will help China to develop from a leading regional power into a crucial global player that is in the centre of change and development.

As a matter of fact, it is likely that by successfully implementing the Belt and Road Initiative and overcoming initial problems, China will be able to lead an increasing share of global supply chains. Thus, BRI can be seen as a cornerstone in China's approach to overcome the middle-income trap[58]. Instead of ending in a position where China is not able to compete anymore the country will be able to lead in the most valuable segments of the production process and use the strong links built through the Belt and Road to create an efficient supply chain in which China is in the centre of the development.

The officially stated objectives of the Belt and Road Initiative are "to construct a unified large market and make full use of both international and domestic markets, through cultural exchange and integration, to enhance mutual understanding and trust of member

---

[58] According to the idea of a "middle income trap", a country has lost its competitive edge because of rising wages. However, it is unable to keep up with more developed economies in the high-value-added market. Thus, the country is stuck with a lower and barely growing Gross National Product. They oftentimes suffer from low investment, slow growth in secondary industries.

nations, ending up in an innovative pattern with capital inflows, talent pool, and technology database."

Like the names suggest, the Belt and Road can be split into two parts, the belt in the title focuses on improving the physical infrastructure along land corridors that roughly equate to the old Silk Road. The road relates to the maritime Silk Road also known as "21st Century Maritime Silk Road". In contrast to the belt, the maritime Silk Road focuses on investment along the sea route corridor.

While it might be easy to see the Belt and Road Initiative as one big project driven by the Chinese Communist Party and the ruling elite in Beijing, it is better to see it as a general concept rather than a specific project. Thus, instead of providing fixed rules and a clear structure, the Belt and Road Initiative remains in many parts unstructured and opaque.

Let us first have a closer look at the developments alongside both, the "Belt" and the maritime Silk Road before finally putting both into a bit more perspective.

Broadly speaking there are three routes that are in the centre of the "Belt" project. The first route reaches all the way from Northwest and Northeast China to the European continent and the Baltic Sea. In-between these two end-points the route is going through parts of central Asia and Russia. Another route goes from Northwest China all the way through central Asia to the Persian Gulf and the Mediterranean Sea. The third and last route goes from Southwest China through the Indochinese Peninsula to the Indian Ocean.

In the centre of the "Belt" is the goal of building and enhancing the Land bridge between Central Asian countries, as well as Russia, Mongolia, West Asia and Indochina. Old and new international transportation routes built the foundation in this ambitious plan that aims to close the economic ties between the countries involved. It thus seems that the idea of economic integration is at the centre of the "One Belt, One Road" project.

The maritime Silk Road follows the trails of Zheng He and runs from China's south to Indonesia, Singapore and Malaysia. Then through the Strait of Malacca via the Sri Lankan Colombo towards the southern tip of India. From there it reaches East Africa, Djibouti, the Red Sea via the Suez Canal and goes all the way to the Mediterranean Sea and Italy.

Chinese money flowing along the new Silk Road is allowing for the development of numerous industrial development zones overseas. In addition to this, new developments of railways and highways along the routes of the old Silk Road are allowing for stronger ties between China, central Asia, and Europe. There are a lot of benefits from closing the ties between the continents as rail transportation is offering a faster alternative to shipping. So far it was the fact that shipping is cheaper that helped it to gain a predominant position in the world of global trade. Therefore, the question remains how competitive the faster alternative of rail transportation is compared to a maritime transportation network. If the cost can compete, the "Belt" with its strong rail network will provide a clear competitive edge for China. If not, the question should be what the future of these projects will be.

In addition to that, the "Belt" will help China secure a reliable source of affordable energy and with a reliable network China will position itself in a less vulnerable position with regard to a potential American naval blockade of the Malacca strait. For example, supplied by different countries and transported through the numerus continental corridors China will be able to obtain fast supplies of natural gas and oil. Thanks to this, China will be able to cover vast amounts of its energy needs and put itself in a better position due to the diversification of its trade partners. The Belt and Road Initiative will help to establish new energy routes towards China, linking together the producers of these resources in Central Asia with the consumers in the hundreds of million-people cities and their many factories across China.

And with all these projects underway, China, already the biggest trading partner for most of the surrounding countries, will become even more important for the economic growth of all of west, south and east Asia.

Thus, while the Belt and Road Initiative looks like an overly ambitious trade agreement between different countries, it can be a key factor in determining the future relations between countries. The idea is that China will at some point lead a value chain that is highly dependent on other countries. For this to happen the Belt and Road Initiative is providing a key cornerstone that lays down the fundamental infrastructure and transportation networks.

In the centre of it all stands the financial system and the state-owned banking system that is a crucial element for transforming the Belt and Road strategy into a real-life success. This state backed financial support will help to navigate the investments into key areas and projects while still allowing for a necessary level of independence. However, it is crucial that, sooner rather than later, China gains better access to global financial markets in order to supplement the domestic measures driving the Belt and Road Initiative.

In the centre of many investments are global container ports and telecommunication networks between Asia and Europe. These projects aim to not only strengthen China's position in the global trade network but also to create an additional, third, digital Silk Road.

At the end of the day, however, the Belt and Road is mainly about global integration and economic cooperation between the participating countries. Physical measures such as roads, ports and bridges are one part of this equation. This equation reaches way further though and also includes the above mentioned telecommunication networks, oil pipelines and power grids.

All these measures and projects will help China to further expand into central and south Asia, Africa and Europe and help to deepen crucial economic ties. It is undoubtable that China has finally emerged as an important global power. The main question that remains is if those countries that do see an alternative to China in either India, the US or another party, will go down the path of joining the Belt and Road project. Or will they choose against increased dependencies on China?

Another example of China's expansion is its involvement in the developing world. Africa places a special role in China's involvement in the developing world and there is an increasing number of signs that China is becoming Africa's new go-to partner as a consequence of years of rising aid, trade and investment in the country. China's aid model is drastically different to the model of many western countries and is mixing aid and commerce, focusing on infrastructure projects and producing sectors rather than on social sectors.

This however is nothing new per se. As a matter of fact, China was an active aid donor in Africa since the 50s and while not as important back then it still manifested early roots around that time. China's influence in Africa grew once the country adopted the so called "Chinese model", meaning their approach of mixing aid with a more general economic engagement.

The key driver for change in China's approach to foreign aid followed from the 1999 "Going Global" policy, which resulted in more commercial interest of Chinese companies in Africa and other parts of the world. Prior to that, despite China's relative poverty, aid programs did not correlate with economic interest.

Looking at it in more detail we can observe that in 1994, the two policy banks (Export Import Bank of China and China Development Bank) were established. EXIM, how the Export Import Bank of China is also known by, provides concessional loans while the China Development Bank (CDB) has a more commercial mandate and offers finance at common market rates. In 2007 the CDB established its first Africa Development Fund (CADF).

Though, while the commercial interest grew, public sectors like healthcare still benefited a lot, with the healthcare sector alone receiving around $\frac{1}{4}$ of all Chinese aid. These public sectors saw only little change despite the "Going Global" campaign.

Thus, the main difference between China and contemporary OECD aid really lies in China's economic interest and increased focus on infrastructure and productive sectors. These are usually relatively small in terms of project numbers but when it comes to size, they are usually the key projects, overshadowing the rest.

Looking at some examples we can see that while China continues its agricultural technology transfer, it has also increased the number of public-private partnerships to finance the projects. Important turnkey projects are now oftentimes funded through concessional loans from China's EXIM bank. In addition to that, China's State-Owned Enterprises (SOEs) oftentimes end up being the beneficiaries of this as they are oftentimes contracted for implementing the projects.

Japan and Korea follow a similar approach, focusing more on infrastructure projects in their foreign aid. They however joined the so called Development Assistance Committee (DAC), while China decided not to. Considering that Chinese SOEs benefit from China's foreign aid programmes it remains open if we will see any changes in this area. It seems very likely that China will increasingly focus on mutual beneficial projects. And while we see increased cooperation between China and other countries through the Belt and Road Initiative it seems unlikely that China will step away from its very beneficial relationship with Africa. This oftentimes is portrayed with a negative undertone in news and media.

However, despite the economic interest in Africa, the country still benefits from China's engagement. At the end of the day it also remains important to remember that China's aid is not purely focused on mutually beneficial programmes but that it still includes vast amounts of medical and educational aid. At the end of the day, we can likely see China to continue its course of increasing interaction with Africa.

# CLIMATE CHANGE

It is hard to deny that climate change is one of the biggest risks of our time and for human society as a whole. Forecasting the future under the impacts of climate change and also identifying effective climate mitigation strategies seems to be an enormous task, considering the high levels on uncertainty and many unknowns.

China, as a matter of fact, has become the world's largest carbon dioxide emitter as of 2017 and its role and responsibility grew over the last years in line with its economic expansion[59].

As if this wouldn't be severe enough, sustainable development and climate change risk are an especially serious matter in emerging countries all over the world. It is in those countries where mass urbanization is occurring, with China being hugely impacted by this as we learned earlier. While this doesn't sound too bad without further context, it is mainly those cities that are exposed to limitations in areas

---

[59] In fact, China is the world's largest greenhouse gas emitter and accounts for almost a quarter of all global $CO_2$ emission.

such as clean water, health care, and living space access. As a consequence most cities face a trade-off between protecting the environment and allowing for basic human needs. This can be due to many reasons such as higher electricity use per unit of GDP, deforestation, and many more. This is why more and more Chinese leaders are inclined to commit to improving sustainability going forward. Some of the key developments include land renewal, green urban planning, and more integrated large-scale recycling. China and it's neighbouring countries become more and more aware of the downsides that come with rapid industrialisation and economic growth.

There are a few factors that differentiate China from many other countries around the globe. With more than 1.4 billion people and an increasing number of people living in urban areas it becomes crucial to consider how China develops its energy grid in the next few years. The consulting firm McKinsey is expecting that China will likely need more than three times as much energy to generate one unit of GDP compared to western countries going forward.

China plays an important role in shaping the future of the world, and government initiatives and policies play a key role in making sure that sustainability is not only promoted but also actively implemented. This includes sustainable financing and a stronger focus on the corporate sector.

We can see that financial institutions and asset managers all over the world increase their focus on using factors such as environmental, social, and governance (ESG) as benchmarks for their investments and paying more attention to each factor on its own.

With financial support in place and increasing demand for innovation, China's cities become successful testing areas for green solutions and sustainable development. This trend is likely to accelerate in the coming years rather than slow down, making it not only a focus from an investor's perspective but also for those that want to drive positive change in the world.

China is already leading in many areas and is ahead of the US in even more. For example, China accounts for half of the electronic vehicle

(EV) sales worldwide and is leading crucial innovation in this area. This also holds for areas like the coal industry, that has been a thorn in China's eye for a long time. And while China's total emission is still high, it is driving innovation in alternative energy sources. As a matter of fact, China has probably done more than most countries in the last decade and played a crucial part in the transition from fossil fuel to cleaner energies.

China is committed to reduce its emissions and is likely to achieve an initial peak sometime between 2021 and 2025. It is very likely that China will also be in a position to help other developing countries to achieve a transition into a more sustainable future, with its vast amount of experience and expertise. It might not be too unlikely that we won't see Germany or the US leading the transition into a sustainable future, but China instead. China is already in a position where it is leading in areas such as hydroelectric and wind power and it might lead in more areas in the next few years. Thus, it is not too surprising that a lot of debate is around how China will moderate future developments in this area. And here again effective policies are in the centre of the debate that will help China to achieve a successful and sustainable future regardless of the future conditions and developments. Targeted policies, together with the necessary investments can help to manage potential future risk related to climate change.

Over the last decade China has moved up the ranks in the fight against climate change and with the help of vast investments and policy actions targeted towards energy efficiency, renewable energy, and the fight against climate change, China is building more and more resilience with every new day and is slowly stepping up to lead the fight against climate change around the world.

The biggest risk at this point is most likely not coming out of China but rather a function of increasing de-globalization and growing tension between the US and China, which in return slows the needed reform process and holds back necessary investments.

# PEACEKEEPER

九

China, together with Russia, has the largest number of land borders with neighbouring countries on the world. Fourteen in total to be precise. We already read about them, but let us repeat them at this point. They are [60] North Korea, Russia, Mongolia, Kazakhstan, Kyrgyzstan, Tajikistan, Afghanistan, Pakistan, India, Nepal, Bhutan, Myanmar, Laos and Vietnam. In addition to that, the East and South China Sea are bounded on the west by Vietnam and on the east by the Philippines and Japan, South Korea and Taiwan.

As you can see from this list, China is not like most countries on this world but instead has exposure to many different cultures, religions and economies.

Going back to the post 9/11 years, the US realized that China would make a great partner in fighting terrorism and function as a peacekeeper for the eastern hemisphere. The hope was that all great

---

[60] Running anti-clockwise from the east to the west.

powers in this world would come together to fight common dangers. However, once George W. Bush's second term started he slowly became more and more sceptical about China and the tension slowly built up as China strengthened its military. As China's dominance in Asia grew the United States slowly started to see China as competitor in Asia that had more than one advantage and the un-competitiveness of the United States in this part of the world slowly turned into the current conflict that we can observe between these two powers. The influence of the United States was waning in the region and as a consequence China was portrayed as a regional hegemony by western Media.

However, while the conflicts between the US and China grew, China's importance as a peacekeeper in the region did not diminish. As a matter of fact, China is probably the most important power to keep the peace in Asia.

If you assume that the international system is in some ways hierarchical, then the logical consequence would be that larger powers have a duty of responsibility towards the smaller powers to create a better and mutually beneficial future. China, as the biggest economy in Asia is increasingly fulfilling this duty and projects such as Belt and Road can also be seen as China's way of creating a mutually beneficial future in which more and more emerging countries in central and south Asia emerge into the developed world.

The smaller neighbours especially profit from the stability and prosperity that a growing and emerging China is slowly bringing to them. China is not a hegemonic power as the United States would want to make someone believe. A hegemonic power would not focus on respect, responsibility and the adherence to principles. Instead, a hegemonic power would neglect these values.

As an outsider it is sad to see that existing powers like the United States are threatened by the fact that a new (and old) not singularly dominant power wants to have a voice on the table and be heard. China's expansions into Africa, the Middle East and other regions did not help to solve this conflict but was instead seen as a new attempt for rivalry for power.

I assume that going forward we have to accept and understand that China has a voice on the table and an important role to play to help levitate the emerging countries in Asia out of poverty and help them with its know-how, best practices and influence to achieve a better future.

Regardless of the outcome of the US-China trade war it seems likely that in the near- and medium-term future China will be the most important power in Asia - not Japan or the United States. China will be the overarching power that will help to keep the peace in the region. Additionally, it will be very likely that China will be the major force behind Asia's economic ascent.

And with all this in mind we should not forget that China has also learned from the many years of foreign occupation from the British and Japanese. Thus, we cannot deny that China is also trying to make sure that something similar will not happen in the next century by manifesting its role on the table. Initiatives like the Belt and Road Initiative make China's neighbouring countries more dependent on it and give China a strong advantage.

I am convinced that neither China nor its neighbouring countries are interested in an armed conflict. Instead, China will follow its path on building economic ties with neighbouring countries rather than attacking them. Trade and economic ties already proved to be the best alternative for Asia. This proved to be the case many times before and in particular during China's success during the Tang and Ming dynasty.

Let's not be too one sided, though. We should not forget to mention that many years of propaganda by the People's Republic of China made the Chinese believe that China is peace-loving and non-threatening power. This however, as we have learned from the South China Sea disputes and the many boarder conflicts, is not always the case. With a history of unstable borders and continuous conflicts, combined with the century of humiliation by the west that China had to experience, we now reached a point where there are suspicions from both sides.

Many Chinese oftentimes see the United States as a hegemony itself that is trying to defend its position and interfere in and prey upon weaker powers. As a consequence some Chinese are of the opinion that China is now in a position where it should regain its power no matter the cost.

For me this is not the base case that we should assume, however. Instead I assume, as previously outlined, that over the coming decades China will actually be of help to other emerging countries to finally emerge. Is there some selfishness in this? Maybe.

# THE NEW NUMBER ONE

I can't lie - up until to this point we spent a lot of time talking about China. Over the last 200 pages we learned about China's past and all its ups and downs. We learned about some aspects of daily life in China today and forecasted how China will develop in the upcoming years. In this chapter I want to advocate for something controversial.

I want to advocate for China being the new number one country in the future.

Oftentimes incorrectly, China is viewed as "a communist state that is missing the many freedoms that the west has to offer". I believe, that people miss to understand and see China as a whole and only see parts of it. Additionally, people oftentimes fail to see how China changed and developed over the many centuries and learned to continuously innovate itself (I do hope that this book helped you to see China as a more diverse country than you would have expected before).

China changed its political system, it's relationships with its bordering countries, and drove innovation in those areas that were seen as necessary. As Deng Xiaoping would have said: "It doesn't matter if a cat is black or white, as long as it catches mice[61]".

Oftentimes people make the argument that China is aiming to dominate the world in hard power terms and will thus do everything to position itself in a way that it can dominate the world sooner or later. Infrastructure projects like the earlier mentioned Belt and Road Initiative, China's foreign policy and other parts of its recent development are used as a reasoning to underline this argument. I hope that with this book I could bring you closer to what I think a more realistic Chinese future might look like. And that is not world dominance but rather a strong position within a globalized world that will help China and its citizens to bring prosperity to everyone in the country and increase the standard of living for as many people as possible. I don't think China has interest in dominating the world. China has interest at being a strong voice on the table that will help the country to be considered.

We have learned in the previous chapter that China will play a more important role in global policy making going forward and also continue to grow its influence on foreign politics. China will inevitably become more interconnected with its trade partners and neighbouring countries and thus not only have an increasing impact on them but also increasingly be the Asian power that will push for peace in this part of the world.

With China's dominance in the world rising we should ask ourselves if we can expect the already high tension between the United States of America and the Peoples Republic of China to intensify or if there is another path for China's future relationship with the US. Will China and the US move further together or drift apart? From what we see now it seems likely that we will see them both drift further apart as China's importance in the region grows. In the previous chapter we

---

[61] "不管黄猫黑猫，只要捉住老鼠就是好猫"

already touched on this issue and it seems likely that we see a de-coupling of countries, followed by increasing nationalism and disruption as a consequence of the trade-war and COVID-19. Instead of having one leading power we will have the US leading the western countries and China its Asian peers. If we expect the tensions between these two global powers to worsen even further, we could even make an argument that it is likely that new confrontations might arise.

In contrast to that, if we would be hopeful and expect tension to be less from here, we could make an argument for a continuous economic growth and a stronger focus on issues of global importance like climate change. This however, seems to be wishful thinking at this point and a further de-coupling seems to be the most likely outcome for the foreseeable future. And while the future seems quite uncertain from here, with arguments for both scenarios sounding feasible, one thing is clear: This might be the most important political development over the next decade.

To put emphasis on how uncertain China's future really is, think back 20 to 30 years and imagine how China used to look like. Would you have thought China would turn into the global power it is today after all the humiliation it had to experience? I would have not and yet we are here talking about a conflict between China and the US, both being key figures in this great game of chess.

It happens only rarely that one single factor determines the way politics will develop and it is just a mere feeling that underlying trends will lead to what I think will happen - a further drifting apart between the US and China. I don't think that this will end in a war, though. I can understand however, that this would make a far more interesting story and great click-bait.

Even with my relatively positive view on China's goals and ambitions I think both countries are at risk of further increasing the tension between one another.

While China might continue to live with Taiwan's special status it might still want to prevent the island from gaining full independence. The hybrid status-quo that we have now might be perfectly fine for the

People's Republic of China for now. And the US on the other side might not want to act against anything else but a direct military threat. However, in this Prisoner's Dilemma both parties might see themselves forced to further increase the tension to maintain the balance.

China, we should point out, would be a clear loser of this increasing tension and de-globalization as it strongly depends on trade. Hence, the Belt and Road Initiative comes in handy to find alternative routes and revenue streams for the country. China is clearly vulnerable to any forms of withdrawal of global goodwill and increased protectionism. This however, might be a price worth paying considering some recent developments (Hong Kong included).

I want you to go away from reading this book with one question in mind. While we can have a rough idea how China's rise might affect the world and spend a lot of time thinking about it, to what extent will China be able to grow its power and what will China's role in the future be?

COVID-19 made it obvious to many observers how severe the impact of disrupted trade is on all countries involved. However, a slow-moving increase in protectionism in the western hemisphere would likely have a similar impact on China and likely lead to tension building up from the Chinese side as a response in the long-run. And while China still seems to be too connected to the rest of the world, not to bite the hands that feeds it, we should never say never.

The Chinese are leading in many areas and their economic success and rise to power is unprecedented. However, the country is struggling the project its way of life abroad and the global audience is usually interested in China for only one reason: selling to 1.4 billion people and making money out of it. So as a consequence of the increasing disputes countries such as India might find themselves as the winner in this war between the US and China. This is not a book about India, though, so let's continue to talk about China's future.

China is now at a key moment that might shape much of its future. While assuming that China will surpass the United States in hard terms it is hard to imagine that China will be able to compete with the US on the same level. Only with a vision of global integration and included in an international order that is multilaterally beneficial will China be able to also lead in soft terms. And for now it seems that this previous international order will likely become a Eurasian order with the world being more divided than before. China could lead the creation of a completely new economic bloc in which western politicians and companies have little say. In this scenario it will be Beijing who is dictating the rules – and the rules of trade are at the sole discretion of the governing body of the People's Republic of China.

Standing up, getting rich, and becoming powerful, are the common three stages people divide the history of the People's Republic of China into. Under Mao Zedong the country stood up. Under Deng Xiaoping China became rich. Now the question is if Xi Jinping will be the one who will make China powerful.

The world order we are moving towards will likely not have the clear centre people are hoping for. Instead, we will see the world more divided than before. The West will likely be only a shadow of what it once was but China's ascent to power is slow and full of hurdles. In the end, China stood up, it got rich, and it will become powerful.

# REFERENCES

Over the years I read tones of research paper, articles, and books about China. In this appendix you find a collection of the works and papers I found the most insightful when writing this book.

Adshead, S. A. M. (2016). *China in world history*. Springer.

Bayles, D. L. (1990). The Reunification of China: An Examination of the Legal Systems of the People's Republic of China, Hong Kong, and Taiwan. *Denv. J. Int'l L. & Pol'y*, *19*, 443.

Bickers, R. (2017). Britain in China: community, culture and colonialism 1900-1949.

Borensztein, E., De Gregorio, J., & Lee, J. W. (1998). How does foreign direct investment affect economic growth? 1. *Journal of international Economics*, *45*(1), 115-135.

Bush, R. C. (2013). *Uncharted strait: The future of China-Taiwan relations.* Brookings Institution Press.

Cai, P. (2017). Understanding China's Belt and Road Initiative.

Chiu, C., Ip, C., & Silverman, A. (2012). Understanding social media in China. *McKinsey Quarterly, 2*(2012), 78-81.

Choe, J. I. (2003). Do foreign direct investment and gross domestic investment promote economic growth?. *Review of Development Economics, 7*(1), 44-57.

Copper, J. F. (2019). *China Diplomacy: The Washington-Taipei-Beijing Triangle.* Routledge.

Cousin, V. (2011). *Banking in China.* Springer.

Creel, H. G. (1953). Chinese thought, from Confucius to Mao Tsetung.

Devan, J., Negri, S., & Woetzel, J. R. (2008). *Meeting the challenges of China's growing cities.* McKinsey Global Institute.

Dirlik, A. (1995). Confucius in the borderlands: Global capitalism and the reinvention of Confucianism. *BOUNDARY 2, 22,* 229-274.

Feng, W., Gu, B., & Cai, Y. (2016). The end of China's one-child policy. *Studies in family planning, 47*(1), 83-86.

Festini, F., & de Martino, M. (2004). Twenty five years of the one child family policy in China.

Greenhalgh, S. (2008). *Just one child: Science and policy in Deng's China.* Univ of California Press.

Gromov, G. R. (1995). The Roads and Crossroads of Internet History, 1999. *URL: http://ftp. sunet. se/wmirror/www. internetvalley. com/intval. html.*

Hu, S. (2007). Confucianism and contemporary Chinese politics. *Politics & Policy, 35*(1), 136-153.

Huang, Y. (2016). Understanding China's Belt & Road initiative: motivation, framework and assessment. *China Economic Review, 40,* 314-321.

Kaltenmark, M. (1969). *Lao Tzu and Taoism.* Stanford University Press.

Kim, E.H., & Singal, V. (2000). Stock market openings: Experience of emerging economies. *The Journal of Business 73*(1), 25-66.

Kirkby, R. J. (2018). *Urbanization in China: town and country in a developing economy 1949-2000 AD*. Routledge.

Ho, D. Y. (1995). Selfhood and identity in Confucianism, Taoism, Buddhism, and Hinduism: contrasts with the West. *Journal for the Theory of Social Behaviour, 25*(2), 115-139.

Ho, K., Wong, S. H. W., Clarke, H. D., & Lee, K. C. (2019). A comparative study of the China factor in Taiwan and Hong Kong elections. In *Taiwan's Political Re-Alignment and Diplomatic Challenges* (pp. 119-144). Palgrave Macmillan, Cham.

Huang, R. (2015). *China: A macro history*. Routledge.

Lan, J., Ma, Y., Zhu, D., Mangalagiu, D., & Thornton, T. (2017). Enabling value co-creation in the sharing economy: The case of mobike. *Sustainability, 9*(9), 1504.

Maspero, H. (1981). *Taoism and Chinese religion* (p. 259). Amherst: University of Massachusetts Press.

Morgan, P., & Zheng, Y. (2019). Old bottle new wine? The evolution of China's aid in Africa 1956–2014. *Third World Quarterly, 40*(7), 1283-1303.

Neftci, S. N., & Menager-Xu, M. Y. (Eds.). (2006). *China's financial markets: an insider's guide to how the markets work*. Elsevier.

Pines, Y. (2014). Legalism in Chinese philosophy.

Powell, J. H. (2017). Jerome Powell: Innovation, technology, and the payments system.

Rosenthal, J. L., & Wong, R. B. (2011). *Before and beyond divergence*. Harvard University Press.

Rozman, G. (2002). Can Confucianism survive in an age of universalism and globalization?. *Pacific Affairs*, 11-37.

Tong, M., Hansen, A., Hanson-Easey, S., Cameron, S., Xiang, J., Liu, Q., ... & Bi, P. (2015). Infectious diseases, urbanization and climate change: challenges in future China. *International journal of environmental research and public health*, *12*(9), 11025-11036.

Tu, F. (2016). WeChat and civil society in China. *Communication and the Public*, *1*(3), 343-350.

Schofield, C. H., & Storey, I. (2009). *The South China Sea dispute: Increasing stakes and rising tensions* (Vol. 24). Washington, DC: Jamestown Foundation.

Schreer, B., & Tan, A. T. (2019). *The Taiwan Issue: Problems and Prospects.* Routledge.

Seligman, S. D. (2008). *Chinese Business Etiquette: A Guide to Protocol, Manners, and Culture in the People's Republic of China.* Grand Central Publishing.

Steidlmeier, P. (1999). Gift giving, bribery and corruption: Ethical management of business relationships in China. *Journal of business ethics, 20*(2), 121-132.

Swaine, M. D. (2015). Chinese views and commentary on the 'One Belt, One Road' initiative. *China Leadership Monitor, 47*(2), 3.

Wang, X. (2016). *Social media in industrial China* (pp. 1-222). ucl Press.

Whitehead, L. (Ed.). (2002). *Emerging Market Democracies: East Asia and Latin America.* JHU Press.

Whitman, J. N. (2018). *An Analysis of the Primary Driver for China's Belt and Road Initiative-Security Versus Economics.* Naval Postgraduate School Monterey United States.

Williams, P. (2008). *Mahayana Buddhism: the doctrinal foundations.* Routledge.

Winston, K. (2005). The internal morality of Chinese Legalism. *Sing J. Legal Stud.*, 313.

Woetzel, J. (2011). How green are China's cities. *McKinsey Quarterly, JANUARY*.

Woetzel, J., Chen, Y., Manyika, J., Roth, E., Seong, J., & Lee, J. (2015). The China effect on global innovation. *McKinsey Global Institute Research Bulletin*.

Woetzel, J. (2011). How green are China's cities. *McKinsey Quarterly, JANUARY*.

Worried About Huawei? Take a Closer Look at Tencent by sarah cook march 26 2019 https://thediplomat.com/2019/03/worried-about-huawei-take-a-closer-look-at-tencent/

Wu, F., & Xue, Y. (2017). Innovations of bike sharing industry in China: A case study of Mobike's station-less bike sharing system.

Yao, S., Luo, D., & Wang, J. (2014). Housing development and urbanisation in China. *The World Economy*, *37*(3), 481-500.

Zakaria, F. (1994). A Culture is Destiny: A Conversation with Lee Kuan Yew. *Foreign Aff.*, *73*, 109.

Zhang, J. (2017). The evolution of China's one-child policy and its effects on family outcomes. *Journal of Economic Perspectives, 31*(1), 141-60.

Zhang, K. H. (2001). Does foreign direct investment promote economic growth? Evidence from East Asia and Latin America. *Contemporary economic policy, 19*(2), 175-185.

Zhou, H. (2011). Confucianism and the Legalism: A model of the national strategy of governance in ancient China. *Frontiers of Economics in China, 6*(4), 616-637.

# THE AUTHOR

Stefan Piech was born in Germany and holds two bachelor degrees; one in law and one in economics. He spent two years at the prestigious Peking University, one of China's top Universities and lived in both, Beijing and Shenzhen.

Printed in Poland
by Amazon Fulfillment
Poland Sp. z o.o., Wrocław